Equalities
and Inequalities
in Family Life

Equalities and Inequalities in Family Life

Proceedings of the Thirteenth Annual Symposium of the Eugenics Society London 1976

Edited by

ROBERT CHESTER
The University, Hull

JOHN PEEL
Teesside Polytechnic,
Middlesborough, Cleveland

1977

Academic Press
London · New York · San Francisco

A Subsidiary of Harcourt Brace Jovanovich, Publishers

ACADEMIC PRESS INC. (LONDON) LTD.
24/28 Oval Road,
London NW1

United States Edition published by
ACADEMIC PRESS INC.
111 Fifth Avenue
New York, New York 10003

Copyright © 1977 by
THE EUGENICS SOCIETY LONDON

Library of Congress Catalog Card Number: 77-74370
ISBN: 0-12-171650-3

PRINTED IN GREAT BRITAIN BY
J. W. ARROWSMITH LTD.,
BRISTOL
TYPE SET BY GLOUCESTER TYPESETTERS LTD.
MERCHANTS ROAD, GLOUCESTER

Contributors

ROMA N. CHAMBERLAIN, *Paediatric Unit, St Mary's Hospital Medical School, Norfolk Place, London W2 1PG, England*

ROBERT CHESTER, *Department of Social Administration, The University, Hull HU6 7RX, England*

D. A. COLEMAN, *Department of Anthropology, University College London, Gower Street, London WC1E 6BT, England.*

ALEX COMFORT, *Institute for Higher Studies, Santa Barbara, California 93105, USA*

ALAN E. H. EMERY, *Department of Human Genetics, Western General Hospital, Edinburgh EH4 2XU, Scotland*

HILARY GRAHAM, *Department of Sociology, University of York, York YO1 5DD, England*

BERNARD INEICHEN, *Department of Sociology, University of Bristol, 12 Woodland Road, Bristol BS8 1UQ, England*

HILARY LAND, *Department of Social Administration and Social Work, Univeristy of Bristol, 12 Priory Road, Bristol BS8 1TF, England*

RICHARD LEETE, *Office of Population Censuses and Surveys, St Catherine's House, 10 Kingsway, London WC2B 6JP, England*

D. H. J. MORGAN, *Department of Sociology, University of Manchester, Manchester M13 9PL, England*

CHRISTOPHER WALKER, *Department of Social Administration, The University, Hull HU6 7RX, England*

MARGARET E. WOOD, *Department of Social Science and Humanities, The City University, St John Street, London EC1V 4PB, England*

Preface

This volume contains the texts of papers presented at the thirteenth annual Symposium of the Eugenics Society. It is the third volume in a trilogy devoted to equalities and inequalities in contemporary society and is concerned with aspects of family life.

Like all previous Symposia volumes its approach is interdisciplinary and we are grateful to the authors of the papers in this volume for their attempts to present up-to-date surveys, commentaries or research reports relating to aspects of their own individual specialisms.

We should like to acknowledge the help of Miss Eileen Walters, the Society's General Secretary, in carrying out the detailed work in connection with this Symposium and its publication and to Mrs Mavis Warnes who prepared the typescripts.

On behalf of the Eugenics Society
ROBERT CHESTER
JOHN PEEL

JUNE 1977

Contents

Changing Patterns
of Marriage and Remarriage

RICHARD LEETE

Office of Population Censuses and Surveys, London, England

The statistical picture from vital registration and successive decennial censuses of population shows that since the turn of the century there has been a wide range of fundamental demographic changes. These include the increase in average life expectancy brought about particularly by the striking reduction in deaths from infectious diseases in infancy, early childhood and young adulthood; the reduction in the size of the average family and the concomitant shrinkage in the size of the average household coupled with the proliferation of small households; the increased participation of married women in the labour force; the upsurge in divorce and changing patterns of marriage and re-marriage. These are not isolated changes but inter-related movements amounting to a revolution in family life.

Of course this demographic revolution has not occurred in a social, political and economic vacuum. The background associated with it has shown rises in the material and physical standard of living; the gradual movement towards relatively full and secure employment as compared with the earlier decades of this century; the building of a Welfare State; advancements in medical knowledge and application; legislation recognizing the equality of women and changes in the permissible grounds for divorce and abortion. Some of these changes are a response to the ideology and actions of particular pressure groups, for example the Feminist Movement. But others, such as the extensive spread of family planning, as distinct from the widespread availability of contraceptives, have few obvious links with any particular organized political movement. Individuals too have modified their views and attitudes towards many social phenomena and switched their preferences to new family life styles. This paper will spotlight the major changes in marriage patterns and see how they link with other changes in family life and with the broader changes in the social and economic structure.

Trends in the Number of Marriages

Figure 1 shows the long-term movements in total marriages and first marriages of both partners. Apart from short term fluctuations, the amplitude of which increased considerably during and immediately preceding and succeeding the major wars, the graphs show that except for the past few years there has been a gradual upward trend. In the first decade of the century marriages averaged 263,000 annually; this rose to 346,000 in the 1930s and to 399,000 in the decade up to 1975, an increase of more than 50 per cent. Although the trend before 1939 was relatively steady the post-war trend has been relatively erratic. Immediately after the war there was a peaking resulting from couples marrying who had delayed in the early 1940s and others marrying younger than previously. In the 1950s there was a relative plateau when children born in the 1930s were passing through the prime marriageable ages. The steady growth in the 1960s, when those born in the post-war baby-boom passed through the prime marriageable ages, has been followed by a sharp downturn in the 1970s. These variations in the number of marriages cannot be explained solely in terms of changes in the age structure or size of the population. They have resulted from the complex interaction of numerous demographic, social and economic factors.

Another feature of this chart is that the distance between the curves,

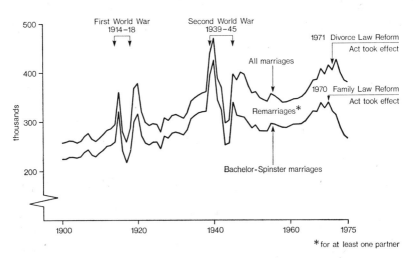

Fig. 1. Marriages 1900–75. England and Wales.

representing re-marriages for at least one partner, increased in the first two decades after the Second World War and has increased even further since the mid 1960s. In the pre-war period the overwhelming majority of re-marriages involved widowed persons but in the post-war era the largest proportion has involved divorced persons. The trend is for a decreasing proportion of marriages to involve a bride and groom marrying for the first time. In 1931 for example 89 per cent of marriages were of bachelors marrying spinsters; this fell to 81 per cent in 1951 and to less than 70 per cent in 1975.

Figure 2 gives an insight into the growth and change in the marital status composition of the male and female populations. In the early decades of this century there were more single females than single males aged 16 and over and also more single persons than ever married (married, widowed and divorced) persons. But with various changes in fertility, migration and mortality resulting in a change in the age structure of the population coupled with changes in marriage patterns, single males aged 16 and over now outnumber single females and ever married persons now increasingly outnumber single persons.

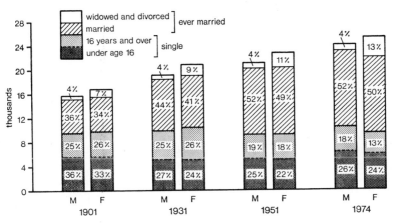

Fig. 2. Persons single and ever married. All ages. England and Wales.

Younger and More Marriages

Before the Second World War marriage was characterized by a relatively late age pattern and a high proportion of women remaining unmarried. Subsequently there has been a striking change in both of these characteristics; people are marrying younger and a higher proportion of women are marrying. In 1931 for example only 26 per cent of females aged 20–24 had married; this rose to reach 48 per cent in 1951 and 59 per cent in 1961 and has since remained near to that level. This movement towards younger marriage is illustrated in Fig. 3 which shows that the average age at first marriage has fallen very markedly since the late 1930s. In 1975 the average spinster, although marrying slightly older than her counterpart in 1970, married two-and-a-half to three years younger than 40 years ago; the pattern for bachelors has followed a similar course, although on average they continue to marry about two years older than spinsters.

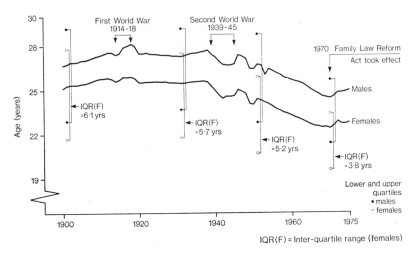

FIG. 3. Mean age at first marriage 1900–75. England and Wales.

These arithmetic means mask considerable variation in the ages of people marrying in a particular year. The lower and upper quartile points indicate the variation of the distribution and an examination of their trend helps to illuminate the fall in marriage age. For spinsters the interquartile range fell by 6 months between 1931 and 1951 and by a further 17 months between 1951 and 1970. The general conclusion, which is the same for bachelors as for spinsters, is that the marriage age of the upper quartile has declined by twice as much as the lower quartile suggesting that the fall in age at marriage is not just the result of a shift of the distribution along the age axis but, in addition, the compression of marriage into a narrower age range.

It is a commonplace that some social groups marry on average younger than others. In 1885 the Registrar General noted that

it is a matter of common observation that among working men marriage is not only more general but takes place at an earlier age than is the case among the upper and middle classes (Registrar General, 1885).

An inverse relationship between social class and marriage age, with brides and grooms in the higher social classes marrying later than their contemporaries in the lower social classes, was confirmed in a special study of the marriage certificates undertaken by the Registrar General in that year. Subsequent censuses of population and numerous other studies have confirmed the persistence of a gradient (e.g. Grebenik and Rowntree, 1963; Glass, 1973; Armstrong, 1974).

Part of the variation arises because the occupational based social classification is in some respects age dependent; entry to particular occupations, for example the medical profession, requires qualifications that cannot be obtained at a very young age. Furthermore, differences in marriage age between the social groups should not lead to the conclusion that there is a causal relationship between the two; marriage age is the result of numerous factors, apart from occupation, although these are shared unequally between the social classes. Indeed social class, although generally assessed on the basis of occupation, is not one-dimensional; the occupation of a person correlates highly with other variables, for example income, education and social origin. Data from the 1971 census indicate that the educational level of a bride is strongly associated with her age at marriage. In 1971 the estimated median age at marriage for spinster brides was 21·4 but there was a two-and-a-half years difference between the most and least educated brides.

In the post-war era there has been a marked decline in lifetime singleness among females. In 1931 some 19 per cent of females remained unmarried at ages 35–44; this fell slightly to 14 per cent in 1951 but by 1974 was at only 6 per cent. However, the current picture disguises considerable variability between the social classes and between groups with different educational attainments as is shown by statistics from the 1971 census (Table IA). For several reasons care should be exercised in

TABLE IA

Percentage of women aged 35-44 ever and currently married. England and Wales 1971

(a) social class; economically active women (per cent ever married)

All	I	II	IIIN	IIIM	IV	V	N/C
89	73	83	88	90	92	97	92

(b) academic level (per cent currently married)

All	A and B	C	D	E
88	74	82	86	90

TABLE IB

Percentage of men aged 35-44 ever and currently married, 1971. England and Wales

(a) social class; economically active men (per cent ever married)

All	I	I I	IIIN	IIIM	IV	V	N/C
90	92	93	89	92	86	76	86

(b) academic level (per cent currently married)

All	A and B	C	D	E
87	91	92	88	86

A and B: Graduates and higher University degrees.
C: Professionals below University but above A-level, eg. Teachers.
D: A-level, HNC and equivalent.
E: Below A-level.

the interpretation of these data, particularly those relating to women. First, the data relate only to persons economically active and who could be allocated to the social classes on the basis of their own occupation. Secondly, the participation of males and females in the labour force is not a random phenomenon; whereas males are concentrated in occupations classified in social class III manual, females are concentrated in occupations classified in social class III non-manual. Thirdly, economically active women aged 35–44 constituted only 57 per cent of all women in this age-group in England and Wales in 1971; of these some 34 per cent were in social class III non-manual, compared with only 1 per cent in social class 1 and 8 per cent in social class V. Fourthly, the composition of each social class is purported to be relatively homogeneous in respect to the skill required to perform the occupations and the educational qualifications leading to them. However, the association between occupation and education may not be as strong for women as it is for men; some married women take jobs of a temporary or localized nature which do not utilize their educational qualifications. Finally, in 1971 only 7 per cent of females and 12 per cent of males in the age-group 35–44 had educational qualifications above A-level.

Table IA shows that there is an inverse relationship between social class of economically active women aged 35–44 and the percentage ever married with the proportion of spinsters highest in social classes I and II, 27 per cent and 17 per cent respectively, and lowest in social classes IV and V, 8 per cent and 3 per cent respectively. Given a relatively high correlation between social class and educational attainment the existence of an association between educational attainment and the proportion of single women is predictable. Table IA confirms this prediction and shows that the difference between the most and least educated groups is substantial. Paradoxically among males the reverse position pertains. The proportion of men aged 35–44 who are ever married is highest in social classes I and II, 92 per cent and 93 per cent respectively, and lowest in social classes IV and V, 86 per cent and 76 per cent respectively (Table IB). Similarly with educational attainment the most highly educated men are more likely to be married than their least educated contemporaries.

There are several possible explanations for these different patterns within and between the sexes, which in spite of the qualification made above are not merely artifacts of the classifications. If men have generally to support their wives, even if only partially, "lower class" men, with lower incomes, may find this more difficult and some may refrain from marrying. It is possible, also, that there is some downward drift, towards lower grade occupations, of men who are frequently or chronically sick and are less likely to marry; thus it may be that a specific strain of men are selected into unskilled manual occupations and out of marriage. Conversely although this process may have operated for women there has been a countervailing force whereby women have been more likely than men to marry partners from a higher social class simply because a higher proportion of women than men pursued unskilled occupations. But why do a smaller proportion of higher educated women marry? It could be that early marriage is a deterrant to seeking further education. A more likely factor is that some highly educated women perceive marriage as a potential obstacle to the advancement of their career opportunities which are wider than those for women with less education; and another may be that men have hesitated to marry women who might be serious contenders for the traditional twin male roles of "chief" breadwinner and "head of household".

Hitherto the main focus has been on marriage indicators of a cross-section of people from different generations. An alternative approach is to examine the marriage patterns of particular generations (Farid, 1976). Figure 4 which shows the proportion of males and females ever married at given ages, again illustrates the principal changes outlined earlier, namely, younger marriages, a higher proportion of women marrying and the compression of marriage into a narrower age range. The more peaked distribution of females born in 1940 is a reflection that over 80 per cent had married by age 25, compared with 48 per cent at the same age of those born in 1900. The chart again illustrates that females marry considerably younger than males. Although 6 per cent of males born in 1940 had married by age 20, some 27 per cent of females had married by that age; both these figures are higher than those for persons born in 1920.

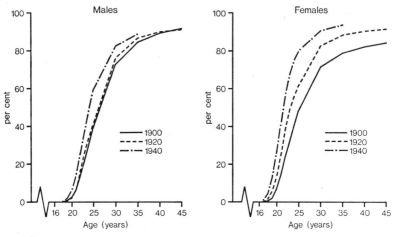

Fig. 4. Percentage ever married—selected birth cohorts. England and Wales.

An important demographic factor associated with the longer-term changes in marriage has been the change in the sex ratio at the marriageable ages. In 1931 there were considerably fewer men than women at the marriageable ages resulting largely from higher net loss of males than females through migration and the high number of deaths of young males in the First World War. In 1931 there were only 85 males aged 20–54 for every 100 females aged 15–49 but by 1951 the imbalance had largely eroded and in 1971 the ratio approached unity. Indeed Fig. 1 showed that there is no longer a surplus of single marriageable women. Before the Second World War the natural excess of boys—each year 106 boys are born for every 100 girls—was largely eliminated by age 16 as a result of sex-selective infant and childhood mortality. But with the reduction in the mortality differential it is now not until about age 50 that there are more females than males. The change in the proportion of males may have helped to produce the slightly greater decline for females than males in the average age at marriage, in addition to allowing a higher proportion of females to marry. However, although a changing sex ratio has been associated with changes in marriage patterns it cannot be concluded that this has been the only factor; the changes should be examined in the wider demographic context and other social and economic factors play a part in the determinants of marriage behaviour.

Why do people marry younger than 50 years ago? In the nineteenth century marriage implied the immediate start of a family. Malthus for "prudential considerations", by which he meant stemming the rate of population growth, advocated that the masses should delay or abstain from marriage (Flew, 1970). For the middle classes the proper time to marry was linked with calculations and considerations as to how the proposed partnership could afford the expense of starting and maintaining a large family and still sustain the pattern of behaviour to which they were accustomed (Banks, 1954; Banks and Banks, 1964). But with the gradual reduction in large families and the spread of birth control practice within marriage coupled with the high degree of acceptance o a small number of children as a desirable family goal such considerations were no longer paramount. Changes in the immediate responsibility to one's spouse have been accompanied by a way of life which allows deferment of procreation following marriage (or even before). On the economic side the period since the Second World War has been until recently one of generally rising prosperity associated with relatively high incomes for young people, tax advantages to married couples where husbands and wives both work and an increased demand for labour which in turn has been accompanied by increased employment of married women. The formal marriage bar imposed in the Civil Service and teaching profession, and the informal bar existing in companies in the private sector, was lifted in the 1940s (Hubback, 1947). Getting married while still continuing to go out to work has increasingly become a pattern of life for younger women (Britton, 1976). Against this background a fall in marriage age could readily occur. And with the increase in the proportion of women marrying there may have been what Professor Glass has termed a "feed-back" effect; as men saw that more women were marrying they themselves became anxious to marry, so the proportion of men marrying increased and this fed back again to women (Glass, 1971). Social class differences in marriage age may be in part accounted for by the earlier independence of manual workers resulting from a generally shorter period of education, apart from apprenticeships, and a quicker rise, particularly amongst the unskilled workers, to an adult rate of earnings.

Recent Trends in First Marriage

There have been two noticeable changes in recent trends in first marriage, namely a delay in the timing of, and a sharp fall in the proportion of brides pregnant at, marriage. Both factors need to be assessed in

TABLE II
Proportion (per 1000) of women who were ever married before attaining selected ages

Birth generation	Age (exact years)								
	17	18	19	20	21	22	23	24	25
1950	18	65	157	283	430	564	665	732	777
1951	19	71	163	305	444	571	665	730	
1952	22	73	189	323	459	579	668		
1953	21	76	190	322	447	555			
1954	23	78	194	322	442				
1955	25	81	194	313					
1956	25	79	185						
1957	23	72							
1958	18								

The figures to the right of the dotted line are affected by the reduction in 1970 of the age of majority.

relation to the impact of the Family Law Reform Act which came into effect in 1970 lowering the age at which a person could marry without parental consent from 21 to 18. In 1970 first marriage rates reached a peak and people married younger than at any time since the beginning of civil registration; subsequently there have been sharp falls in first marriage rates at most ages. In 1975 the lowest rates since the Second World War were recorded and there has been a rise in marriage age.

The cumulative effects of recent changes in first marriage rates can be seen in Table II. The figures show that the proportion of women married by the time they reached 19 was slightly smaller for the 1956 generation (18·5 per cent) than for the two preceding generations (19·4 per cent in both cases). The 1954 birth generation, who reached marriageable ages after 1970, showed the highest proportion (19·4 per cent) married by the time they reached age 19 but subsequently showed a slower cumulative rate of marriage between the ages of 19 and 21 than the immediately preceding generations. Thus the immediate effect of the Family Law Reform Act was to produce increased marriage rates at under age 20, but this was mainly a bringing forward of marriages because there have not been commensurate changes in the proportions married by ages 21 or over. The decline in marriage rates since 1973 has led to lower proportions ever married for most generations compared with the preceding generations at the same ages. Whether this fore-shadows a significant trend towards later marriage, as has been seen for instance, in the United States of America in recent years, or is merely a temporary phenomenon, in response to recent economic constraints, are questions which only the passage of time will answer. Of course the recent increase in singleness amongst the young could lead to a per-

manent decline in marriage. An American commentator has observed
that

> just as cohorts of young women who have postponed childbearing for an
> unusually long time seldom make up for the child deficit as they grow
> older, so also young people who are delaying marriage may never make up
> for the marriage deficit later on (Glick, 1975).

People may try, and like, alternatives to marriage, and the "fashionable"
alternative is extra-marital cohabitation, probably much more frequent
now than for the past 100 years.

Brides Pregnant at Marriage

The relationship between pregnancy and the timing of marriage is
complex. Although some marriages may occur as a result of an unplanned
pregnancy often couples have already planned to marry and conceive
confident that a wedding is imminent. In other cases only one partner
may intend or hope to marry and risks conception in order to induce the
other to accept marriage. In practice there is no way of assessing
accurately from the available statistical data the relative importance of
each of these circumstances.

From the mid-1950s the proportion of brides who were pregnant on
their wedding day increased until by 1967 some 22 per cent of all
spinster brides, but 38 per cent of those aged under 20, had a birth that
was pre-maritally conceived. Since 1967, however, there has been a
sustained reduction in the number and proportion of brides pregnant at
marriage (Fig. 5), and in 1974 only 14 per cent had a birth that was
pre-maritally conceived, the lowest percentage since the early 1950s.
The decline in the number of pre-maritally conceived births has been
proportionately more marked for brides aged 18–22. Indeed the large
fall for those aged 18 years and over contrasts markedly with little or no
change for the 16 and 17 years old. The reduction for the age range
18–22 may be associated with earlier marriage facilitated by the
Family Law Reform Act—there has been no corresponding reduction
in Scotland where the Act does not apply. But in so far as the fall in
pre-maritally conceived births occurred at roughly the same time as
changes in abortion provisions and contraceptive services it is impossible
to quantify the relative importance of the various factors associated
with the decline.

Overall figures of pre-maritally conceived births conceal considerable
differences between the social classes. Table III shows that there is an
inverse relationship between the proportion of legitimate first births
that are premaritally conceived and the social class of the father ranging
from 8 per cent of first births to couples in social class I to 43 per cent of

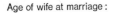

Age of wife at marriage :

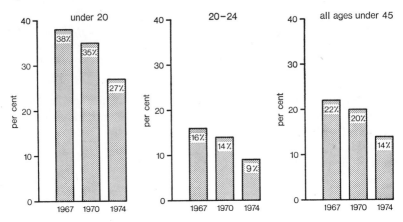

FIG. 5. Percentage of first marriages with pre-maritally conceived live births. England and Wales.

first births to couples in social class V. The break between the manual and non-manual groups is particularly pronounced. However, the interpretation of these figures is complex since they confound the effects of age and occupation: the age composition of persons in social class I and II implies that pre-marital conception rates, which are highest for women aged under 20, will be low among women of the higher social classes. Moreover, although the timing and practice of birth control differs between the social classes one cannot conclude that differences in pre-maritally conceived births is the causal factor in differential social class age at marriage. It may be for example that there is a custom among particular social groups to conceive once a wedding has been planned.

TABLE III
Percentage of legitimate first births premaritally conceived; by social class of father. (England and Wales 3.3% sample 1970-72)

Total	I	II	IIIN	IIIM	IV	V	AF
24	8	12	17	27	32	43	25

Re-marriage—Changes in the Supply
Changes in the pattern of re-marriage since the Second World War must be seen against marked changes in the characteristics and composition of the supply of persons on the re-marriage market. The key factors that have affected the supply are, first, a significant fall in the number of deaths to married persons where the surviving spouse is aged

TABLE IV
Deaths and divorces   England and Wales

	Deaths 000s	Married men aged 15–59 Divorces 000s	Married Men 000s	Death rate per 100,000	Divorce
1951	44	28	9000	487	313
1961	46	25	9430	487	260
1964	46	34	9493	481	353
1970	43	56	9505	452	592
1974	39	107	9492	414	1127
		Married women aged 15–59			
1951	30	28	9414	314	302
1961	26	25	9884	259	252
1964	25	34	9943	254	343
1970	25	57	10070	246	567
1974	23	108	10025	232	1081

under 60 and, secondly, a steep rise in the number of divorces (Leete, 1976). Table IV highlights some aspects of these key factors. Since the 1960s divorce has ended more marriages where the spouse is aged under 60 than death; divorces have quadrupled since 1951 and continue on an upward trend. However, death rates of married persons aged under 60 have declined steadily since the 1950s, although the rates for men are still nearly twice as high as those for women.

The post-war uptrend in divorces which became noticeable in the 1960s and more marked after 1971, when the Divorce Law Reform Act

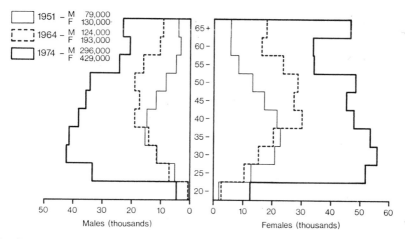

FIG. 6. Age structure of the divorced population. England and Wales.

took effect, together with changes in the annual pattern have caused major changes in the size and age structure of the divorced population. Figure 6 illustrates the magnitude of these changes at three points in time. Between 1951 and 1964 the divorced population increased by more than 50 per cent to 317,000, the growth confined largely to ages above 45; between 1964 and 1974 the divorced population more than doubled but the growth was most pronounced at ages below 45. Thus the divorced population now has a much younger age structure than during the 1960s. This change is the result of the rapid rise in persons divorcing at younger ages and at shorter durations of marriage; it also reflects younger marriage in the 1950s and the greater propensity to divorce. At the older ages the greater mortality of males leads to an increasing disparity between the numbers of divorced women and of men. The imbalance is accentuated by the greater tendency of divorced males than of divorced females to re-marry. In 1974 there were 296,000 divorced males, half of whom were aged under 43·4 years compared with 429,000 divorced females, half of whom were aged under 44·3 years.

The male and female widowed population shows similarities with the divorced population, for example imbalance between the sexes, growth in the older ages, largely reflecting the increasing extent to which widows outlive widowers. In 1951 there were 314 widows for every 100 widowers, by 1974 this ratio had risen to 423. But in contrast to the divorced the widowed population has aged since 1951 reflecting the older age structure of the inflow resulting from increasing expectation of life. In 1974 the median age of widows was 72·1 years compared with 68·1 years in 1951; the corresponding figures for widowers were 72·2 years and 70·6 years respectively.

Rise in Re-marriage

Against this background it is not surprising that weddings involving re-marriage for one or both partner(s) are becoming increasingly numerous or that the trends in the patterns of re-marriage for widowed and divorced persons should differ markedly. From 1951 onwards there was a steady decline in marriages of widowed persons but in the mid-60s and the early 1970s there was a levelling of this trend and even a slight rise; but marriages of divorced persons have risen substantially, particularly since 1970. In 1951 the number of widowed persons re-marrying was roughly the same as the number of divorced persons re-marrying; but in 1964 for every 100 widowed persons re-marrying there was 125 divorced persons re-marrying and by 1974 this ratio had increased to

350. The average widowed person is now about 5 years older at the time of re-marriage than in 1951, but the average divorced person is now slightly younger; these trends are expected given the changes in the age structures outlined above.

Rates of Re-marriage

Over the past fifteen years there has been little change in the re-marriage rate of widowed persons; but although there has been a sharp rise in the number of divorced persons re-marrying there has been remarkably little change in the rates of re-marriage of divorced persons (Fig. 7) in

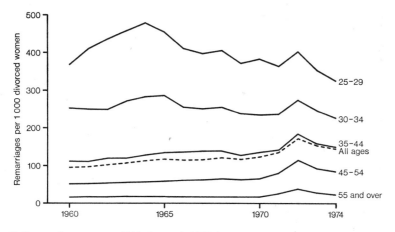

FIG. 7. Remarriage rate per 1000 divorced, 1960–74. England and Wales.

spite of the very large inflow into the divorced population. Thus the increase in the number of re-marriages is due to the increase in the population "at risk" rather than an increased tendency to re-marry. Indeed at the younger ages there have been small falls in the re-marriage rates of the divorced.

The peak rate of re-marriage for divorced persons is at the younger ages where the annual inflow into the divorced population is proportionately largest, implying re-marriage for a high proportion of young divorced persons occurs within a few years of divorce. At every age the re-marriage rate for divorced persons exceeds that of widowed persons and that of males of either status exceeds that of females. The difference between the re-marriage rates for males and females is due to the greater propensity of males than females to re-marry.

There can be little doubt that there is now a greater social acceptability of ending marriages and re-marrying. However, many demographic, social and ecomonic characteristics of persons re-marrying remain unknown. For instance, is there a greater likelihood of re-marriage for persons with or without young children? What are the characteristics of persons who never re-marry? What are the average intervals between widowhood, separation, divorce and re-marriage, and what is the structure of the new family when a re-marriage occurs? Research into some of these questions is currently being undertaken in OPCS using statistics derived from marriage registration, divorce records and through special surveys.

Acknowledgement

I am pleased to acknowledge the assistance and encouragement of my colleagues in OPCS during the preparation of this paper. OPCS is not responsible for the views expressed; responsibility is mine alone.

References

Armstrong, A. (1974). *Stability and Change in an English County Town*. Cambridge: Cambridge University Press.

Banks, J. A. (1954). *Prosperity and Parenthood*. London: Routledge and Kegan Paul.

Banks, J. A. and Banks, O. (1964). *Feminism and Family Planning in Victorian England*. Liverpool: Liverpool University Press.

Britton, M. (1976). Women at work. *Population Trends*, 2, 22–25. London: HMSO.

Farid, S. M. (1976). Cohort nuptiality in England and Wales. *Population Studies*, 30, 137–151.

Flew, A. (Editor) (1970). *Malthus T. R. An Essay on the Principle of Population*. Harmondsworth, Middx.: Pelican Books.

Glass, D. V. (1971). The components of natural increase in England and Wales. In *First Report from the Select Committee on Science and Technology: Population of the United Kingdom*. London: HMSO.

Glass, D. V. (1973). *Numbering the People*. Farnborough, Hants.: Saxon House.

Glick, P. C. (1975). Some recent changes in American families. *Current Population Reports*, 52, p. 23.

Grebenik, E. and Rowntree, G. (1963). Factors associated with age at marriage in Britain. *Proceedings of the Royal Society*, 159B, 178–197.

Hubback, E. M. (1947). *The Population of Britain*. Harmondsworth, Middx.: Penguin Books.

Leete, R. (1976). Marriage and divorce: trends and patterns. *Population Trends*, 3, 3–8.

Registrar General (1885). *Forty-Eighth Report of the Registrar General*. London: HMSO.

Assortative Mating in Britain

D. A. COLEMAN

Department of Anthropology, University College London, London, England

Introduction

Assortative mating sounds a chill and clinical name for what should be an agreeable recreation. Indeed now that I have spent some time looking at previous work on the subject I realize that I should have chosen the more dignified term "assortative marriage" for my title. For, to my great regret, I have found little systematic information on the biological or social similarity of partners still engaging in the illicit hurly-burly of the chaise-longue as opposed to those committed to the peace and quiet of the marital bed. But in Britain at any rate about 95 per cent of the population finally marries so data from marriages will be an almost universal, if not a wholly typical sample of behaviour.

Definition of Assortative Mating

Assortative mating or marriage is a social process whereby sexual partners who are similar in some character or characters are chosen more frequently than would be expected by chance. I intend to discuss this phenomenon from a genetical as well as from a social-psychological point of view, partly because I am interested in it for its genetical consequences, partly because the genetical aspects of assortative mating are much better defined than the sociological ones and may even serve as a rough model for them. To me it is an interesting topic because, although the genetical, social and psychological aspects are potentially strongly connected with each other, little work has been done on their integration and indeed the whole topic seems to have been ignored by British sociologists except where it has to do with class or politics. In this paper I will look at some of the genetical, psychological and socio-logical theory of assortative mating and its supposed causes and consequences, and briefly review some data which has been collected relating to biological, psychological and social similarities of married people, particularly in Britain.

Genetical Aspects of Assortative Mating and its Distinction from Inbreeding

Assortative mating, as a genetical phenomenon, should be distinguished from the related phenomenon of inbreeding. Inbreeding is the preferential marriage of relatives—either because they are relatives; relatives being preferred to non-relatives in the marriage market; or because mobility and population size are so low that all potential mates are relatives of one sort or another.

Both inbreeding and assortative mating will increase the proportion of homozygotes in the population and reduce the proportion of heterozygotes; that is, there will be more individuals in the population where the two genes at each position on the chromosomes will be of the same type rather than of different types. In association with this there will be a corresponding increase in the variability of the population, conventionally measured by the mean squared deviation from the population average of each character, or "variance". But with inbreeding, the increase in homozygosity and variance will apply to all genes and to all characters. Assortative mating by contrast does this only for those characters for which the partners are similar and to no others, unless they are very closely linked. Furthermore inbreeding *always* has genetical consequences, simply because the partners have ancestors in common. But in assortative mating the characters for which the pair are similar may owe nothing to gene similarities and in that case the genetical consequences of their choice will be nil.

In general assortative mating increases population variance more than inbreeding does, to an extent depending on similarity between mates and the degree of genetical control of the variability of the character. If the correlation r between mates is 0·25, a typical figure for height, with a heritability approaching 100 per cent, then variance is increased by one-eighth after one generation and one-third eventually. As the variance between families increases, the variance within families declines and relatives become more like each other. For example, if we take the correlation for husband and wife for measured intelligence as 0·5 and assume it has a heritability of 0·8, then the correlation coefficient between one parent and child will rise to a value of 0·6. By comparison, the theoretical maximum under random mating, which would not be reached for a character with heritability less than 1, is 0·5 (Crow and Felsenstein, 1968).

Why Does Assortative Mating Matter from a Genetical point of view?

There are three related reasons why assortative mating makes a difference to the genetical and evolutionary status of human populations.

(1) In general, by increasing the inheritable variance of the population it thereby must increase the potential rate of natural selection.

(2) Although it cannot of itself directly cause gene frequency change, it may facilitate changes of gene frequency and will certainly lead to changes in genotype frequency, often for conditions of medical and eugenic interest. It will particularly increase the frequency of conditions caused by rare recessive alleles leading, in an extreme case, to an increase in frequency of a condition from q^2, a very small number under conditions of random mating, to q, the gene frequency itself, which will be relatively a much larger number (Spuhler, 1968). Mild examples of this are assortative mating for deafness and possibly for some forms of mental illness (Penrose, 1944). Gene frequency may be changed indirectly by assortative mating because in many cases individuals with a given condition often marry others similarly affected where otherwise they would be unlikely to marry at all, in which case the gene frequency would decline.

(3) Even a relatively small increase in population variance may increase considerably the relative frequency of individuals with extreme values of a character; the very bright, the very stupid, the very tall, short, black or white. For socially visible characters this may have considerable importance on the polarization of society. The only estimate which I have seen on its relative importance is that of Burt and Howard (1956) whose authenticity is currently being questioned. This was that assortative mating was responsible for 18 per cent of total variance of height in the UK and for 20 per cent of variance in IQ.

If we accept the values given by Burt and Howard then it follows that the variance of IQ in the population has been raised to 1·25 times its previous level. For a variable such as IQ, which is approximately normally distributed with mean 100 and standard deviation 13·42 (the variance reduced by 20 per cent), then the ratio r between the number of individuals with any given IQ value x under the original distribution, compared with the number having the same absolute value under the new distribution with increased variance is $r = 0.8944 \exp \dfrac{(x-100)^2}{1800}$.

(I am indebted to Mr F. L. Brett for the derivation of this formula.) It follows that the number of individuals with IQ 100 after the increase of variance due to assortative mating is 89 per cent what it had been previously; the number with IQ 130 would be 147 per cent of the previous number, and those with IQ 145 would be 275 per cent. The same increases apply of course to those with IQ 70 and IQ 55 respectively—the average ability of the population does not change.

Assortative mating involving visible genetic characters which act as markers or labels may well preserve distinct communities and possibly their attitudes, values and resentments, which would otherwise have ceased to exist or to be distinguishable from the rest of the community such as the blacks in the USA and other immigrant groups (Taeuber 1934).

What Empirical Evidence Exists of Assortative Mating for Biological Characters?

ANTHROPOMETRIC BIOLOGICAL VARIABLES

Karl Pearson (1903) was the first in Britain (and I think the first anywhere) to undertake a systematic investigation of the problem in the general context of inheritance and evolution. From a large self-measured sample he derived correlation coefficients of 0·28 for stature, 0·20 for maximum span of the arms and 0·20 for the length of the left forearm as well as lesser cross-correlations between different characters.

These values have in general been confirmed in many subsequent enquiries on Western populations as the examples in Table I show. But it is rather remarkable that when many other visible metrical and

TABLE I
Selected examples of assortative mating for biological characters

Character	Population	Product-moment correlation between husbands and wives	Author
Stature	UK	0·28 ±0·02	
Maximum span of arms	UK	0·20 ±0·02	Pearson (1903)
Length of left forearm	UK	0·20 ±0·02	
Head length	Scottish	0·14	Willoughby (1933)
Bizygomatic breadth	Scottish	0·01	Willoughby (1933)
Cephalic index	Scottish	0·01	Willoughby (1933)
Colour of skin	Sikh	0·349 $p < ·001$	Roberts and Kahlon (1972)
Colour of skin	US Negro	0·37	Taeuber (1934)
Colour of hair	Swedish Lapp	0·28 (C) $p < ·001$	Beckman (1962)
Colour of eyes	Swedish Lapp	0·00 (C) $p = ·99$	Beckman (1962)
Stature	Oxfordshire	0·23 $p < ·001$	
Weight	Oxfordshire	0·15 $p = 0·04$	
Hand length	Oxfordshire	0·22 $p = 0·004$	Harrison *et al.* (1976)
Hand breadth	Oxfordshire	0·08 $p = 0·279$	
Head length	Oxfordshire	0·08 $p = 0·346$	

physical characteristics have been tested, the correlation coefficients hardly ever exceed 0·25 and in some cases are so low as to be not significantly different from zero.

In comprehensive summaries by Susanne (1967) and Spuhler (1968) the results of tests for assortative mating in relation to almost every imaginable anthropometric character and index are presented. Very few exceed 0·25. Exceptions to this generalization tend to come from unusual samples; for example a sample of 107 infertile couples from hospital records compiled by Pomerat (1936) who show $r = 0·63 \pm 0·04$ for height, and 0·40 for trunk length. The other exceptions are mostly odd and spasmodic: xipho-epigastric length in 653 Sardinian couples ($r = 0·46 \pm 0·021$ (Tomici, 1939)), length of forearm in Ann Arbor is ($0·43 \pm 0·01$ (Spuhler, 1968)) and length of little finger (Spuhler, 1968). In such a large collection of correlations, a small number of high and significant values would be expected from chance alone. With a sample size of 100, about 4 correlations of 0·25 would be expected by chance from the approximately 350 samples described in these summaries. Many of the measurements are components of height, in others the correlation remains even after adjustment has been made for height.

NON-ANTHROPOMETRIC BIOLOGICAL VARIABLES

The similarity between mates for non-anthropometric variables are often stronger than those reported above, for example eye-colour and hair colour. Expecially in earlier work these characters have not been measured on an interval scale and are estimated by non-parametric measures of association such as the coefficient of mean squared contingency C ($\sqrt{\dfrac{X^2}{X^2 + N}}$) or a rank-order correlation such as Spearman's r_s or Kendall's T. Values obtained for these coefficients may not be comparable with values obtained from Pearson's r. One rather interesting non-anthropometric variable with a biological component is length of life. The first careful study was presented by Pearson, Weldon and others in 1903 from cemetery records in Yorkshire and Oxfordshire. Both gave correlations for length of life of husband and wife of $0·22 \pm 0·02$ and $0·25 \pm 0·02$ respectively. Care was taken to ensure that burial practice did not create the association, and indeed the more complete written records of the Society of Friends showed an almost indistinguishable correlation of $0·20 \pm 0·02$. By contrast a sample from London graveyards, thought to be biased for sepulchral homogamy because only those members of transient urban populations who died temporally and geographically close to their spouses could be recorded as spouses, gave the much higher value of $0·42 \pm 0·02$. Pearson's ingenious statistical manipulation enabled the effects of one partner's demise on the other's life-chances to be allowed for, and the effect of this was claimed to be negligible. But the data collected were so restricted that it could not allow the adjustment for social class, known to be a very important associate and probably determinant, of length of life. If this effect is real, then the effect of this assortment, in view of the apparent hereditary influence on the length of life, may be quite important in increasing variance in expectation of life in the general population. Class difference in expectation of life will accordingly be maintained by, as well as being partly responsible for, this phenomenon.

Fertility

If assortative mating existed for fecundity then the rate of change of gene frequencies could thereby be influenced directly by marriage patterns. Several studies have reported correlations for fertility of mates, measured indirectly and at one remove by the size of their sibship. In societies practising contraception fertility measured in this way may be meaningless in relation to biological fecundity, merely reflecting instead norms of family size and contraceptive practice associated with social class. When the association between sibship size, class and education is controlled, (Warren, 1966) assortative mating for sibship size becomes very weak. Beckman and Elston (1962) have shown that apparent assortative mating for sibship size can be accounted for by a temporal change in mean family size.

Can Assortative Mating for Physical Characteristics be Accounted for by Assortative Mating for Age or Class, or by the Secular Trend?

It has been suggested that the very high level of assortative mating for age might explain a good deal of the correlation for biometrical characters between husband and wife, especially when most surveys take a cross-section of the population including couples of every duration of marriage. A number of physical measurements, such as stature, are known to change with age in a regular fashion throughout the life of the individual. Also, couples may tend to grow alike in weight as a result of sharing the same marital environment for many years. But these changes tend to be slight except at extreme ages, and the notion has been tested and rejected by Willoughby (1933), Griffiths and Kunz (1973) and others.

But another possibility has been put forward by Beckman (1962). It may be that secular trends may have introduced the element of variability into samples where demographic or metrical traits show apparent assortment. For example, Pearson's data on length of life were taken from tombstones covering quite a long period of time in the nineteenth century when length of life was increasing. Because of the strong assortment for age at marriage, spouses will tend to come from the same marriage cohort, and because of the secular trend they will be more similar to each other, than to others in the sample, for length of life. Similar considerations may apply to such variables as stature and its anthropometric components, which have experienced considerable regular secular increase since the mid-nineteenth century, in all classes of society (Tanner, 1962). Beckman suggests that the low correlation of about 0·2 for biometric traits is rather suspiciously uniform and may be due largely to the combined effects of strong association for age at marriage and the secular trends. Clearly this is a statistical trap to be beware of in samples where several marriage cohorts are included. But in fact a number of samples where the data are broken down by year of marriage, or which consist of one marriage cohort only (Harrison *et al*, 1976) still show a strong association. To remove this objection completely, birth cohorts should be studied; as marriage cohorts will include some respondents married in their 30s and 40s as well the majority married in their 20s. These objections do not apply to such characters as eye colour, or to many social characteristics.

Does the Process of Assortative Mating have a Genetical Basis?

The last genetical problem to be considered is whether there might be any evidence that a preference for mating with perceptibly similar phenotypes in man might be described as "innate".

In biology in general some form of assortative mating, to ensure breeding only within the same species, is essential for the maintenance of species as discrete Mendelian units and consequently essential to their continued adaptiveness to their ecological niches. Observations on the behaviour of many forms of animals make it clear that this selection often arises from rigid behaviour patterns of a kind which seem to be inherited. Indeed these "isolating mechanisms" might be regarded (Knight *et al.*, 1956) as the most important part of the species' genotype as they permit continued adaptation to a specific environment without introgression of alien and nonadaptive genes. But does this selectivity extend within species, as well as between them? It has certainly been shown (Godfrey, 1958) that interfertile but geographically separated subspecies of small mammals will mate preferentially with their own group, and similar results are known from studies of domestic fowl (Lill, 1968). Furthermore, homogamous behaviour can be selected for in insects (*Drosophila*) and the isolating mechanisms thereby set up appear able to maintain themselves indefinitely (Thoday,

1964). But other studies suggest that, at least in the higher animals, such preferential mating is the result of habituation to a given distinguishable form in early life, a process akin to imprinting, and is not an inherited preference (Kilham and Klopfer, 1968). It is highly unlikely that inherited preferences could exist with respect to selected polymorphic characters or polygenic traits within an interbreeding species and it is difficult to imagine any selective advantage to the species in doing so. The variability of the intensity and of the characters subject to assortative mating in our species enable us to reject the possibility altogether.

Social Aspects of Biological Assortative Mating

If we assume that there is no innate basis of assortative mating we are left without an adequate explanation of the reasons for assortative mating for physical characters. The individual correlations for size of foot, length of middle finger, etc., are usually "explained" as components of a general assortment for physique. But passing the problem over to a general assortment for size does not necessarily solve it. It is not at all clear exactly why men choose women of similar height to themselves. This rather low correlation is usually taken as a self-explanatory fact, but if you think about it this sort of similarity is rather weak compared to the strong dissimilarity of sexual choice. What is it that induces a weak feeling for general somatic resemblance on top of a very strong taste for somatic difference? It is a taste for one's own general body image, a need to facilitate conversation and other forms of intercourse, a desire to avoid derision—which itself would require explanation? Physical attraction is well known to be very important in choosing a mate, more so to men than to women. There also seems to be considerable consensus on who is considered attractive, members of either sex being equally reliable judges, and there is some evidence that newly married couples tend to be alike in their degree of their physical attractiveness (studies on these problems are summarized in Wilson and Nias, 1976). But the definition of "attractiveness" and the study of its genetical aspects seem not to have advanced much since Galton's day (Galton, 1883).

Assortative Mating for Psychological Characters

As far as psychological characters are concerned, the studies on assortative mating fall into two rather unnatural categories. The first are those conducted by social psychologists in connection with social psychological theories of mate-selection, such as those of Winch described below. On the whole these have not concerned themselves with the genetical aspect of the problem, neither have they been followed much by workers in Britain. On the other hand there have been a number of enquiries in Britain and in which US have been concerned with empirical evidence of choice for cognitive ability and personality. Some of these have emphasized the genetical aspect of these variables.

Psychological Theories of Mate Selection

WINCH AND COMPLEMENTARY NEEDS.

Winch and his colleagues (Winch *et al.*, 1954) have made a notable, if deviant, attempt to account for marital choice in social psychological terms.

They propose that mate selection can be usefully considered on at least two levels. The first level is the restriction of choice to a "field of eligibles", that is, members of the opposite sex who have been encountered by the subject and who are regarded as potential mates because of their compatibility of class, background, educational level, intelligence, interests and values. This is the "filter" of homogamy. But within the "field of eligibles" the personal psychological tastes and needs of the individual exercise a final choice not investigated at all by the crude correlations of homogamy studies. Winch hypothesized that for the satisfactions of needs, such as dominance/deference, abasement/ autonomy, a different and complementary personality is required. His results (Winch, 1955) are not entirely clear cut, but it was claimed that a sufficient proportion of those correlations which were statistically significant were negative, to support the hypothesis and to discredit the notion that homogamy obtained for these characteristics. Some workers have questioned Winch's work (e.g. Bowerman and Day, 1956), others have come to a different conclusion (Sindberg *et al.*, 1972), but without much effect on his original views (Winch, 1967). Kerckhoff and Davis (1962) have given support to a hierarchal system of mate selection. One of the few studies in England directed to this problem (Nias, 1975) showed no tendency for married couples to have complementary personalities and, indeed, showed no clear association of any sort between the personalities of the partners. One of the difficulties is that it is perhaps unreasonable to expect all of the large number of sub-divided needs, identified by Winch, to be subject to the requirement of "complementarity" in all couples at all times and at the same strength. One might expect that the presence of the need might itself vary with personality. As far as I know there have been no studies of this need-structure of personality from a genetical point of view. If these "needs" are consistently found in studies of human personality then they might be expected to have a non-zero heritability. A pioneer student of the problem of psychological needs stressed what he thought to be their "instinctual" nature (Maslow, 1955), and many of the conventional dimensions of personality measurement devised by psychologists, such as the measures of extraversion and neuroticism of Eysenck's Personality Inventory, have been shown by twin studies to have significant heritabilities in our culture at least (Shields, 1962; Canter, 1969). The evidence about their correlation between mates is more equivocal, as we will see later.

The theories of Winch and his colleagues should properly be described as being theories of disassortative rather than of assortative mating. They should thus have the interesting property of reducing variance, either genetical or social or both, for the characters concerned and thus perhaps reducing the potential for such disassortative mating in the future. There is another specifically genetical point which might be raised in this context. An important aspect of symmetrical disassortative mating is that it must very often involve selection against the most frequent form and consequently a change in gene frequency if the condition is heritable. If strict and symmetrical disassortative mating is practised in a population where there are 70 per cent of one form and 30 per cent of the other, then clearly 40 per cent of the population will be unable to find a mate if the rules are obeyed. The gene frequency will consequently change to 50–50, independently of any "intrinsic" effect on fertility of the variation. Thus the frequency in the population of individuals with alternative forms of the same "need-variable" must be more or less equal if Winch's model is to work and to be detectable. But unless these attitudes are socially or genetically inherited there seems no obvious reason why they should be equal in frequency.

Assortative Mating for Measured Intelligence and other Aspects of Personality

Measured intelligence shows one of the highest correlations between spouses of any variable with genetical connotations. The usual value obtained is between 0·3 and 0·5 (see Table II). This character is interesting for two or three related reasons. First because twin studies and other investigations show that in our society IQ has a high heritability between 0·5 and 0·9 (Erlenmeyer-Kimling and Jarvik, 1963). Consequently a high degree of assortative mating will have an important effect on the population variance of genotypes as well as phenotypes. The second is the role of intelligence in certain cybernetic theories of social mobility and marriage exchange (Young and Gibson, 1963) whereby an important genetical element is introduced into a social process. The notion here is that the association of class with IQ is a functional one, that high IQ is necessary for successful performance of the jobs which are classified into the higher social classes, despite the inevitably imperfect association between genes and ability, ability and job, and job and class. Because of the necessarily imperfect genotypic correlation between parents and offspring, many children will be born into backgrounds unsuited to their native abilities and will tend to rise or fall in the class structure according to their IQ (Gibson and Mascie-Taylor, 1973), so maintaining class differentials by a dynamic process of recruitment and demotion. Assortative mating comes into this in this way: by decreasing familial variance it tends to increase the chances of a child's IQ being compatible with his father's class and thereby making it more likely that he will remain in that class (assuming that it is an appropriate one to begin with). Or, put another way, by increasing the correlation between parents and children it acts to reduce the level of social mobility needed to maintain the system, and would thereby lend more permanence to the stratification of society.

Some Recent British Studies on Assortative Mating for IQ

One of the most recent major studies of psychological aspects of assortative mating was carried out in Oxfordshire. The whole population in a group of villages was tested for IQ and other psychometric variables. As Table II shows, the overall correlation for IQ was 0·279 which breaks down into 0·343 for verbal IQ and 0·141 for performance IQ—rather low values by previous standards. While the magnitude of

TABLE II
Correlation between spouses for psychometric variables

Character	Population	Correlation between spouses	Aithor
Total IQ	English	0·388	Burt and Howard (1956)
Total IQ	US	0·60	Jensen (1969)
Total IQ	Oxfordshire	0·279 $p < 0·001$	
Verbal IQ	Oxfordshire	0·343 $p < 0·001$	
Performance IQ	Oxfordshire	0·141 $p < 0·01$	Harrison et al. (1976)
Neuroticism	Oxfordshire	0·015 not sig.	
Extraversion	Oxfordshire	−0·049 not sig.	
Inconsistency	Oxfordshire	0·159 $p < 0·001$	

correlation coefficients for spouses both locally born, or both born outside the area are similar to those for the whole sample, the value for couples where one partner is local and one non-local is not significantly different from zero. This is a surprising finding, but it is duplicated by data from the same survey relating to stature.

OTHER PSYCHOLOGICAL CHARACTERISTICS

Harrison's survey also tested spouses for three components of personality: neuroticism, extraversion and inconsistency, from the Eysenck Personality Inventory. Rather surprisingly, no correlation between spouses was detected either for neuroticism or for extraversion, nor is their cross-correlation with IQ significant. But there is a significant positive correlation for "inconsistency", and this is negatively correlated with the spouses IQ, and they suggest that this value of "inconsistency" might be becoming stronger in more recent marriages. Strong class differences for the strength of correlation for IQ were found, but not for personality variables. As Table III shows, social classes I and II shared a high and significant correlation for IQ, classes III, IV and V did not.

TABLE III

Assortative marriage for IQ and personality by social class

	Social class		
	I II	III	IV V
Husband's social class at marriage			
n	108	141	94
Verbal IQ	0·650	0·386	0·295
Performance IQ	0·242	0·168	0·081
Total IQ	0·553	0·323	0·155
Neuroticism	0·104	0·008	0·244
Extraversion	−0·013	0·197	0·157
Inconsistency	0·288	0·299	0·197

From Harrison *et al.* (1976).

Social Aspects of Assortative Mating

Social theories to account for the causes and consequences of assortative mating for socially defined characters seem less explicit and precise than genetical models. No suitable general mathematical model seems to exist to describe it. Therefore the social consequences of assortative mating for social characters cannot precisely be predicted.

REASONS FOR BEING INTERESTED IN THE SOCIAL ASPECTS OF ASSORTATIVE MATING

In general terms the main reason for being interested in assortative mating for social characters is, I suppose, similar to the reasons for our interest in the genetical side of the process; because it may be expected to increase variance, tends to polarise the population and produce more individuals with extreme values for characters than would otherwise be the case. Here of course the increased variance is "social" variance for acquired attributes. For example, ethnic, class and religious divisions, and maybe even the generation gap, are in part maintained and even increased by assortative mating. Children brought up in homes where parents share tastes and preferences, are presumably more likely to grow up sympathetic to these attitudes rather than to those of the average population outside the family. This may conserve socially inherited attitudes much more strongly than any genetical mechanism: there is no social equivalent to the random assortment and independent segregation of genes. One example is the inertia seen in voting behaviour. Husbands and wives tend to be alike in political preference. Insofar as this is due to assortative mating it is probably in most cases a secondary consequence of assortative mating for class, to a lesser extent perhaps also of assortative mating for the personality dimension "tough-minded/tender minded". Among activists assortative mating for political views may be likely to be direct and strong, at least in defining the "field of eligibles". Whatever the cause of the assortative mating, the effects on "inheritance" is strong. It is well known (Butler and Stokes, 1969) that one of the best predictors of an individual's voting tendency is that of his father, (the association being much higher than for any biological variable) and this effect is greatly reinforced if both parents vote the same way. This high association seems well explained by the conservation of traditional attitudes strengthened by assortative mating. And these often survive one generation at least of social mobility. This seems a more convincing model of electoral preference than that of rational choice—surveys regularly reveal widespread ignorance of issues and personalities among the electorate (Rose, 1976). The learned acquisition of attitudes, shared and reinforced by both parents will presumably help to preserve the tendency to assortative mating in the next generation and hence to conserve the whole system.

Assortative Mating for Social Characters

THEORIES OF THE SOCIAL ASPECTS OF MATE SELECTION

Homogamy through Propinquity
Most research on the social aspect of assortative mating—especially on theory—has been carried out in the United States. Many studies there (starting with Bossard, 1932) have noted and described the close

proximity of the places of residence of couples married in American cities. The different areas of cities in the USA (and elsewhere) tend to be occupied by different ethnic, racial or class groups, many of which will also have their own characteristic patterns of religious affiliation and educational level. It is therefore proposed by some authors (Catton and Smircich, 1964) that much, if not all, the observed homogamy for these characters, is caused by the localized nature of social and other activities which may lead to marriage. The localization of activity is held to be a consequence of very general rules of human behaviour (Zipf, 1949). Activity is localized not through any preference for the proximity of similar people, but simply because time and effort spent travelling is rather spent on needs near to home and is only expanded on mobility when these needs cannot be satisfied locally. Hence it is likely that young people will encounter and marry others similar to themselves rather than different from themselves. There are many difficulties with this point of view, particularly in reconciling it with what is known about mate selection in Britain.

To begin with one must ask why these distinctive ecological areas exist in the first place. They have developed, presumably, because people like living near to those with attitudes and life styles similar to their own rather than different. In other words, because of a form of assortative choice. In some cases this will arise because they cannot live anywhere else through poverty or because of restrictions set upon them—but this cannot apply to all or even most of the areas in question. For ethnic minorities there is certainly some evidence that assortative mating for ethnic status, and also for geographical propinquity, has increased in the past (Kennedy, 1943) but this is a special case which should not necessarily be extended to more homogeneous societies.

But studies in Britain (Coleman, 1973), France (Girard, 1964) and elsewhere show that marriages in higher-class categories, while increasingly strongly assortative for class, are much *less* "propinquitous", despite the smaller size of middle-class areas compared with working-class residential areas. Not only does their lifestyle make the middle classes more generally mobile, but the small size and the wide scatter of middle-class enclaves may require them to move about more in search of a suitable mate from their own class. Furthermore many couples meet for the first time in circumstances which are likely to take them away from their own local areas—namely at work (13 per cent—especially middle-class respondents) and at dance halls (about 25 per cent—especially working-class respondents). Only about 10 per cent of the respondents to one survey specifically mentioned that their first encounter was in their own "local area" (Pierce, 1963).

Norms and Values Related to Social Class

More orthodox (if vague) sociological ideas (Jacobsohn and Matheny, 1963) — I do not think they can be called theories, are based on the normative assumptions that individuals feel happier in the company of those who share as many attitudes and habits with them as possible and are therefore likely to marry someone who satisfies these needs; at the very least so that there will be no friction to spoil a romantic relationship based on more personal and less quantifiable attractions. In British society anyway, class seems the best general predictor of all manner of social and educational attributes and hence class endogamy may be used to summarize homogamy for various other characteristics. But this sort of approach, although plausible. lacks substance without an adequate, theoretical background in the psychology of social behaviour.

Assortative Mating for Social Characters

To begin with I will describe the general pattern using a comprehensive American survey, whose findings have been more or less confirmed by other work, and then examine the more patchy results for Britain which are available. One of the most general in scope of the American studies was carried out on 1000 middle-class Chicago residents who were engaged to be married. (Burgess and Wallin, 1943). The subjects were interviewed to elicit as wide a sample as possible of social factors and attitudes for which homogamy might be investigated. Responses for each of the 51 characters were coded into three or four categories and a contingency coefficient (C) calculated from the X^2 value of the table. (Maximum C for a 3×3 table is 0·816, for a 4×4 table 0·866). It should be added that the contingency coefficient simply gives an indication of the extent to which observed frequencies on the cells of a table depart from the expected values derived from marginal frequencies. The nature of the deviation must be determined by inspection of the table, and the value of C cannot easily be related to other measures of association. But especially with categorical variables there is no other summary measure of association taking all categories of a pair of variables together. C has then been widely (if not too widely) used in homogamy studies. All but 6 of the 51 social characteristics yielded significant values of C reflecting a positive association between the partners.

The highest values were for the cluster of characters related to religious affiliation and belief, with a mean value of 0·54. "Family background", that is occupational class and income of parents, was also high at 0·38, followed by "courtship behaviour" (age at meeting and previous engagements) at 0·33 and ideas about marriage and desired family size (0·31). Homogamy for "social participation" that is membership and activity in organizations, was somewhat weaker at 0·24 and strength of family bonds, attachment to parents, number of siblings, etc, was relatively unimportant with an average C of 0·12. The authors felt that the highly individual nature of some of these correlations lent support to the notion that individuals actively preferred mates similar to themselves, rather than the homogamy arising simply through propinquitous marriages. In that particular context another American study might be mentioned briefly. Responses by another set of engaged students (Kerckhoff, 1963) showed that the proportion homogamous with their fiancés for occupational class, education and religion was considerably greater than the proportion homogamous with the first and second boyfriends, while the level of homogamy for population size of place of origin which might reflect the effects of propinquity, or at least the similar values of similar sorts of home area, declined markedly.

Assortative Mating for Social Characters in Britain

ASSORTATIVE MATING FOR SOCIAL CLASS

One of the first surveys carried out in Britain, was of soldiers and their wives (Woodside, 1946) which revealed the now familiar patterns of similarity in class, age at marriage and interests. This study was particularly distinguished by its comparison between the marriages of hospital patients who were ill for purely "physical" causes and subsample who displayed "neurotic" symptoms. The level of homogamy in the "neurotic" cases was distinctly lower than among the control group. It is difficult to say if this is because the neurotic were bad at selecting partners, or whether choosing the wrong partner causes neurosis. The first general sample specifically concerned with problems of social mobility and assortative mating for class in Britain was carried out in 1949–50 by the Population Investigation Committee (Glass, 1954). As Table IV shows, the data provides a strong relationship between social class at marriage, measured on the Hall-Jones scale of socio -economic class (Hall and Jones, 1950). The class of the bride at marriage is, of course, that of her father. The table shows that assortative mating for class is very much stronger at the upper end of the class scale than in the middle, with raised indices of association also at the bottom end of the scale. The index of association is the ratio of "observed" to "expected" numbers where both husband and wife are in the same category. It should be mentioned that with this index, which has been widely used in the description of such surveys, the magnitude which such a ratio can attain depends on the relative frequency of the category in question. If a category comprises 50 per cent of both sexes in the population then

it is impossible for assortative mating to raise its "index of association" above a value of 2. By contrast, a category comprising 10 per cent of both sexes in the population can have a maximum index of 10.

TABLE IV

Comparison of indices of association, distinguishing four social groups and three periods of marriage

Social Group of origin	Year of Marriage			
	Before 1915	1915–39	1940–	All cohorts
I	7·764	6·381	6·558	6·639
II	1·633	1·425	1·406	1·458
III	1·218	1·174	1·156	1·177
IV	1·863	1·678	1·482	1·643

Results of Tests of Significance

A. All indices are significantly different from unity.

B. *Between Marriage Cohorts*
   There are no significant differences.

C. *Between Social Groups*

Before 1915:	There is no significant difference between Groups II and IV. All others differ.
1915–39:	All differ significantly.
Since 1939:	There are no significant differences between Groups II and III and II and IV. All others differ.
All cohorts:	There is no significant difference between Groups II and IV. All others differ.

From Berent (1954).

These tendencies are seen also in a more recent sample which was also carried out by the Population Investigation Committee, in 1959–1960 (Coleman, 1973). In a national sample of 2338, class endogamy, measured on a modified form of the same Hall-Jones scale, gave a contingency coefficient of 0·494 and a rank order correlation of 0·223 for husband's job by wife's father's job at marriage, and a higher contingency of 0·559 with a rank order coefficient of 0·204 for husband's father's job by wife's father's job. These figures may mean rather more if they are translated into the ratios of the "index of association" as shown in Table V. Overall, the ratio is only 1·449, but when analysed class by class, very striking differences are revealed. A ratio of 11·37:1 in socioeconomic class I declines to low values in the middle of the range among clerical and skilled manual workers and rises again somewhat through semi-skilled to unskilled manual workers, as in the previous survey.

As we have been using so much American data it might be interesting at this stage to compare these results with those from the USA. Some

TABLE V

Assortative mating for socio-economic class. Ratios of observed to expected numbers where both partners come from the same class.

	1930–39	1940–49	1950–1960	Total
1	14·8	6·9	12·2	11·4
2	6·1	11·1	6·3	8·2
3	3·0	2·0	2·4	2·5
4	0·8	1·2	1·0	1·0
5	1·9	2·9	2·4	2·4
6	1·2	1·3	1·2	1·2
7	1·4	1·4	1·4	1·4
8	1·4	2·1	2·8	1·9

N.B. the totals include data from 1920–29 whose sample size is to small for separate tabulation.

recent data (Hope, 1972) show that none of the American class categories has a predictive value of more than 4·2 per cent, that is, the percentage accuracy of predicting membership of a class for one partner when that of the other is known. But in recent British samples discussed by Hope this value varied from 14·2 per cent for men of social class I to 3 per cent for men of social class IIIm, rising again to 6·5 per cent for men in social class V.

Changes in Class Endogamy Over Time: The PIC and Reading Surveys
There is a little evidence that assortative mating for class may be relaxing slightly. The overall index of association in the earlier samples declined from 1·419 for the 1890 birth cohort to 1·290 for 1920–1960, which is not significant. If the homogamy values for the PIC sample are looked at separately for each decade's marriage cohort from 1920 to 1960 the contingency coefficient, and to a less regular extent the rank order correlation coefficient, declines rapidly at first but then more slowly (see Table VI). But the earlier cohorts are deficient in the older ages at marriage, and over the period the relative frequency of the different classes has changed, so the changes may not wholly be due to changes in marriage behaviour. A more recent survey of 946 marriages in Reading between 1972 and 1973 showed a rather weaker association with class, with a lower contingency value of 0·405 and a rank order correlation of 0·278. But this should not be taken as clear evidence of a further decline in class endogamy as the sample is local, not national, and the class categories used are not the same as those used in the PIC survey.

Assortative Mating for Religious Affiliation and for Strength of Religious Feeling
In both these samples quite a high value is obtained for assortative

TABLE VI

Changes in the intensity of assortative marriage for socio-economic class
1920–1960

Marriage cohort	X^2	df	p	N	$\sqrt{\dfrac{X^2}{N+X^2}}$	Kendall T
1920–29	146·9	56	<0·00001	237	0·619	0·283
1930–39	302·1	56	<0·00001	578	0·586	0·243
1940–49	260·8	56	<0·00001	648	0·536	0·217
1950–60	267·6	56	<0·00001	683	0·531	0·279

mating for religious belief. Some of this association may follow from different religions being localized by class and by religion—both of which there is strong homogamy. Thus Anglicans predominate in the middle class, Roman Catholics are over-represented in the working class, with Noncomformists somewhere in the middle. I have grouped together Methodists, Baptists and Noncomformists. Noncomformists predominate in the Celtic fringe, Roman Catholics in city ghettos and Anglicans in rural England.

The strength of the departure from expected frequencies for religion is given its most important contribution by Roman Catholic marriages and to a lesser extent by those of Methodists and other Noncomformists. There is a clear deficit of marriages between Anglicans and Catholics— doubtless for class reasons—but only a very small deficit between Anglicans and Methodists. As far as the very small numbers allow any comment, there is a very notable deficit of marriages between Non-conformists and Catholics, presumably indicating strong theological

TABLE VII

Assortative mating for religious affiliation.
Ratios of observed to expected numbers where both partners belonged to
the same religion

	P.I.C. Marriage Survey 1959–60	Reading Marriage Survey 1974
Church of England	1·3	1·1
Church of Scotland	8·9	—
Roman Catholic	4·5	2·4
Noncomformist	4·5	4·0
Other Christian	21·0	12·0
No religion	—	9·5

N.B. No ratio has been calculated in cases where the expected number is less than 1.

distaste among the pious and, in general, perhaps a tendency to live in different areas (although this cannot be the reason in the localized Reading sample).

Note the rather low value for Anglicans and the higher values for Roman Catholics and Nonconformists. In the Reading sample, though, the highest ratios are shown by the small numbers of those who claimed no religion at all, and the even smaller number belonging to minority Christian sects as such the Salvation Army and the Seventh-Day Adventists. By the law of averages it is very difficult for members of minority religions to marry a co-religionist unless both are regular church attenders or their residences are very localized. In Britain both of these may pertain for the Catholics, the former only for the others.

Strength of Religious Feeling

One of the strongest associations between the partners is for strength of religious feeling. In the Reading survey, the couples were asked if they went to church regularly, occasionally or never. This threefold division gave a contingency coefficient of 0·5511 with a rank-order correlation of 0·503. The greater part of this assortment for "devotion" comes from regular churchgoers. They marry each other 3·73 times more than expected by chance compared with occasional churchgoers for whom this ratio is 2·37 while the non-churchgoing mass marry each other only 1·36 times more often than chance would suggest.

As might be expected, the strength of assortative mating for specific religious adherence depends on this regularity of church attendance. These data are for Anglicans, Roman Catholics and Nonconformists only to ensure comparability of tables. Where both partners are regular churchgoers the contingency coefficient for religious affiliation is 0·627 (max. 0·816), where both partners are occasional churchgoers $C = 0·389$, but where both partners never go to church the departure from expected frequency is still highly significant with $C = 0·306$. This rather surprising result is presumably a consequence of the religious association of the different classes and regions of the country.

Changes over Time in Assortative Mating for Religious Affiliation

Finally the PIC and Reading data were used to see if there was any sign that the strong assortment for religion might be declining with time. The overall contingency coefficient from 1920–1960 was 0·844. This declined from a high correlation of 0·884 in the 1920s fairly regularly to a low correlation of 0·806 in the 1950s. Each of the C values was highly significant but it is not certain whether the trend itself is significant. But some confirmation comes from the Reading marriages of 1972–73.

These are technically comparable because the tables have the same number of categories, although the distributions are different (the Reading sample includes hardly any Scottish Presbyterians). The C value for Reading is 0.666, a clear decline in religious endogamy which may be at least representative of the South East for the early 1970s if not for the whole country (see Table VIII).

TABLE VIII
Changes in the intensity of assortative marriage for religious affiliation 1920–1973

Marriage cohort	X^2	df	p	N	C	Source
1920–29	883·1	49	0·00001	254	0·881	Marriage Survey 1959–60
1930–39	1672·7	49	0·00001	631	0·852	Marriage Survey 1959–60
1940–49	1894·1	49	0·00001	693	0·855	Marriage Survey 1959–60
1950–60	1357·3	49	0·00001	731	0·806	Marriage Survey 1959–60
1972–73	744·9	49	0·00001	945	0·666	Reading Marriage Survey 1974

Assortative Mating by Age at Marriage

Assortative mating for age at marriage is very high in all Western samples. For the Reading sample, which included second marriages as well as first marriages, the correlation was a very high 0·9. The strength of the correlation for age varies in an odd way with social class, as Fig. 1 shows. When the husband is in social class I the association is very high (0·821). This declines through class II (0·587) to reach a low in class IIInm of 0·350. In the manual working class the strength of the association begins to rise again (0·587) in class IIIm 0·761, in class IV and 0·752 in class V. All the individual coefficients are highly significant at the 0·001 level of probability and this non-linear association seems to be real, but it is not clear to me why it should exist.

Assortment for Age at Marriage and Fertility

Berent (1954) suggested that class differentials in fertility might be increased through the interaction of assortative mating for class, and the higher mean ages of marriage in the higher classes. But the effect is probably slight. Fertility may be affected in a more general way by positive assortative mating for age at marriage. But the effect is probably slight because male fecundity does not decline rapidly with age in the same way as a woman's does (although coital frequency may do so) and as long as husbands are not too aged fertility is unlikely to be substantially impaired. This is especially true in Western society where fertility is already much lower than biological fecundity because of contraception. Of course if young women were unable to remarry after their aged husbands died then this might have a more important effect and if the sexual energies of younger men are supposed to be directed to older women then the effect will be compounded. Some such arrangement is found in a few simple societies—the Samburu of East Africa and especially the Tiwi of Australia. The elders reserve for themselves the young women and the young men have to make do with older women, but pressures of sex are known to make these arrangements less than watertight. It has been suggested that if fertility is thereby lowered then this would be an adaptive response for nomads.

Assortative Mating for Terminal Age of Education (t.a.e.)
The highest level of association between spouses, after age at marriage, is in terminal age of education (t.a.e.) This might be thought to be a

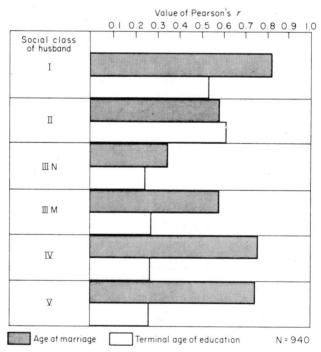

FIG. 1. Reading Marriage Survey, 1974. A comparison of levels of assortative mating within each social class for age at marriage and terminal age of education.

very good index of the sort of skills which have been acquired and consequently of occupational status, and also of the sorts of interests and values of the individual. Insofar as educational level seems to carry a prestige of its own somewhat separate from that of class, the association between spouses for this variable might even be expected to be stronger than that for class.

The correlation between spouses changes considerably on the class scale as Fig. 1 shows. This presumably reflects the more demanding requirements for most of the occupations in the higher social classes and is in line with the findings on assortative mating for IQ mentioned earlier. It may also reflect differences in priorities between the classes in the criteria for choosing a mate. In husbands of social class I and II the correlations for t.a.e. are 0·526 and 0·611 respectively, which is not a significant difference. This declines to the lowest value in class IIInm (0·244) and remains at approximately the same level in the manual working class (0·281, 0·268 and 0·259 in classes IIIm, IV and V. respectively). Differences in assortative mating for t.a.e. then, seems to distinguish the "middle" class from the "working" class better than the other variables we have looked at. The low value for class IIInm may reflect its rather heterogeneous nature; it includes everyone from sales-man to draughtsmen and will include some in clerical jobs who will soon move into management, and many others who will not.

As far as trends over time are concerned, the 1949–50 survey showed that the index of association for each of four educational categories (elementary, secondary, further and higher) declined markedly in the three latter groups, from the pre-1915 marriage cohort to the post-1940 cohort (Berent, 1954). I do not myself think this necessarily shows any change in assortment—the relative frequencies of those attending education after the elementary stage has increased enormously since then and this must have an effect on the maximum index value possible. Unless they are corrected, these indices should not really be compared for tables with very different relative frequencies in each class from one table to another.

Assortative Mating and Marital Status
The Reading survey, unlike the PIC survey, includes remarriages as well as first marriages. Not surprisingly there is a strong assortative mating for previous marital status. Bachelors tend to marry spinsters (ratio of observed: expected 1·116) divorcés to marry divorcées (3·193) and the strongest association of the three is that widows tend to marry widowers (11·23). Some sort of pattern would be expected on age grounds alone: the mean ages at marriage of bachelors, divorcés and

widowers being 24, 44 and 56. These data enable us to see if assortative mating for various characters becomes stronger or weaker when people marry for the second (or third) time. Fig. 2 indicates that in general, assortative mating is stronger among partners of whom both have been married before, compared with those of whom neither have been married before. If true, this may tend to raise assortative mating levels in time as in 1973 remarriages made up 28 per cent of all marriages in England and Wales, compared with 15 per cent in 1960 and 9 per cent in 1938 (Glass, 1976).

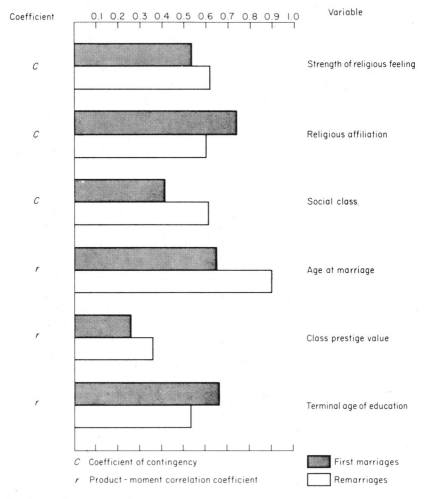

Fig. 2. Reading Marriage Survey, 1974. A comparison of assortative mating in first marriages and remarriages.

In the Reading first marriages, correlation for age at marriage is much weaker (0·648) than where both had been married before (0·901) although in the latter case there must be a restriction on age groups merely by sampling only divorced people. The mean age for the remarriages is 48·2 and 44·1, whereas for the first marriages it is 23·5 and 21·0 for husbands and wives respectively. The husband's class at meeting has a much higher correlation with the wife's father's class among the remarried than among the first marriages, whether it is measured by the Goldthorpe-Hope scale (Goldthorpe and Hope, 1974) ($r=0·363/r=0·260$) or by Registrar General's social class ($C=0·604/C=0·408$). Remarried people are more alike in their churchgoing habits than those who are married for the first time ($C=0·618/C=0·544$), partly because a much higher proportion of them go to church (47 per cent of the remarried men compared to 32 per cent of the bachelors). It might then seem odd that assortative mating for religious affiliation is less among the remarried ($C=0·604/C=0·738$) but this is at least partly due to the fact that more of the remarried describe themselves as Anglicans (81·1 per cent of men to 73·4 per cent) and there are only half as many Roman Catholics among the remarried, so the scope for selection is less. The only important departure from this tendency for the remarried to be more alike than the first married is in the important character of terminal age of education ($r=0·534/r=0·655$). This difference is difficult to account for as the remarried sample is rather more middle class (40/98 nm) than the first marriages (208/599). Two intervening decades of educational change may be responsible: mean values of terminal age of education are 15·4 and 15·5 for the remarried, and 16·8 and 16·6 for the first marriages. Assortative mating for t.a.e. may simply be getting stronger in successive age-cohorts—an argument which can be deployed against the other differences, of course. But the balance of evidence seems to be that those marrying again choose someone more like themselves.

A Multiple Variable Approach to Assortative Mating

All these correlations between spouses are summarized in Fig. 3. But it is not sufficient just to list these separate correlations. We already know that many of these variables are strongly correlated with each other. Some of them will be primary criteria by which choice is actually made, some of the other correlations may be incidental and secondary associations are derived solely or partly from their associations with the determining factors. For example we know that social class, for which homogamy is quite strong, is also associated with age at marriage, religion, geographical mobility and other variables for which assortative choice is made.

One approach to isolate the determining factors is to eliminate the effects of one or more variables at a time by controlling for the variance for which they are responsible, by the techniques of partial regression and correlation and their extensions. This approach was pioneered by Warren (1966) in the USA, but it only can be used for normally-distributed variables. Other multivariate approaches have concentrated on comparisons of generalized distance from population means for sets of biometrical characters (Susanne, 1975) but these are not so suitable for measures which are parametrically different.

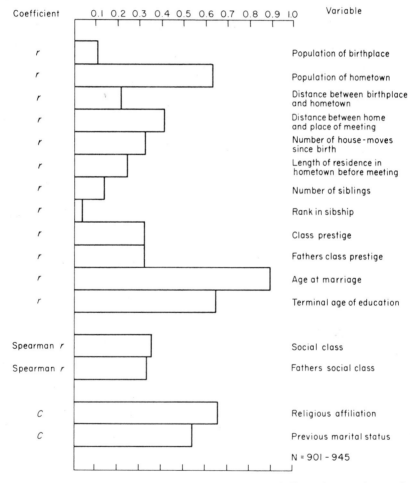

FIG. 3. Reading Marriage Survey, 1974. A summary of indices of assortative mating.

Partial Correlation Analysis of Assortative Mating for the Reading Sample
Figure 4 shows how this technique can be used on three sets of variables
which are thought to be related to each other and which all show positive
assortment in married couples. Assortment for age at marriage is seen to
be very little dependent either on assortment for terminal age of education or on the correlation between husband's and wife's class, class here
is measured by the Goldthorpe-Hope prestige scale. When controlled

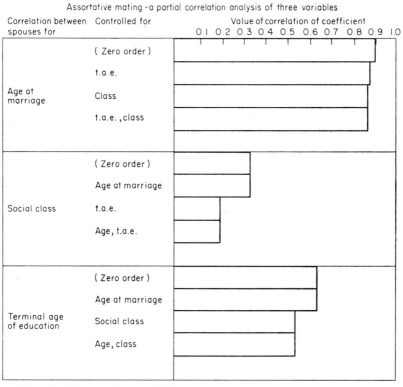

Fig. 4. Reading Marriage Survey, 1974.

for these two correlations the coefficient for age at marriage is reduced
only very slightly from 0·900 to 0·875. Terminal age of education shows
slightly less independence. When allowance is made for the correlation
between the spouses' classes and their age at marriage, the correlation
for t.a.e. declines from 0·647 to 0·547. Almost all this reduction is caused
by the elimination of the correlation for class. Lastly, the correlation
between the prestige values of the husband's job and his wife's father's
job is substantially reduced from 0·338 to 0·204. All this reduction is
obtained by removing the correlation for t.a.e., that for age at marriage

has no effect. This little analysis shows that of the three variables the correlation for age at marriage is almost completely independent, applying over the whole social class scale and also irrespective of terminal age of education (we know in fact that it has a curvilinear relationship with class), but the other two are related. We conclude from this that similarity of t.a.e. without similarity of class is a more decisively direct determinant of marital choice than is similarity of social class without similarity of t.a.e. Or put another way, that similarity in educational attainment makes it easier to marry across class barriers than does class similarity in the face of educational incompatibilities.

Factor Analysis of Assortative Mating

With a large number of variables, partial regression is cumbersome and the results too voluminous for easy comprehension. Another approach is through factor analysis. The point of factor analysis is to take a large number of variables relating to a set of individuals and to extract from them a smaller number of (unobserved) independent variables, the "factors", which can be manipulated to be as independent (uncorrelated) from each other as possible and which summarize concisely as much as possible of the total variance of all the variables. These factors are generated by taking into account not only the relative importance of the contribution to total variance of each of the original variables, but also of their inter-correlation. Variables which seemed to be important at the beginning of the analysis may be shown to owe most of their prominence to their association with others. The rather experimental results of such an analysis are given in Fig. 5.

I hoped that clusters of factors of three sorts might emerge: (1) factors which represented similarities between the partners and therefore typifying the marriage as a unit; and factors peculiar to husbands (2) and to wives (3) separately, and therefore characterizing the marriage as two distinct individuals. The relative importance of factors of similarity, and of dissimilarity in the marriage could be assessed by reference to the respective amount of total variance which they account for (the variances of each variable are all standardized to make them comparable in this way). The "joint" factors show variance between marriages caused by different pairs of husbands and wives being different from other pairs—the partners varying together. The other factors related separately to husbands and to wives reflect differences between husbands and other husbands, for example, independently, of the wives' variability and also variability, within the marriage. Whether a factor is "joint marital" or "individual" can be decided by seeing whether the variables which "load" strongly on each factor in turn are predominantly from both partners, or from husband or wife

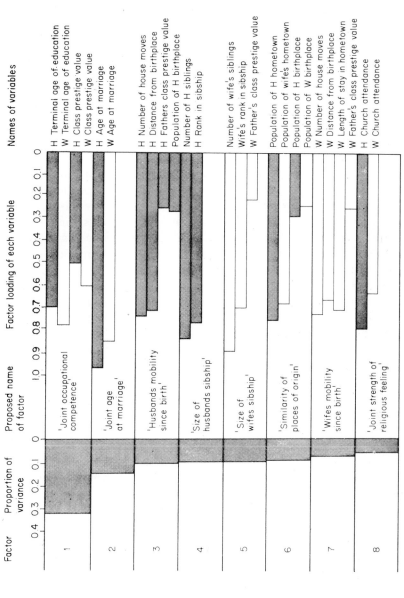

FIG. 5. **Reading Marriage Survey, 1974. Factor analysis of selected variables involved in assortative mating.**

alone. This particular factor approach (there are several) is intended to maximize the difference between factors with respect to the variables which "load" strongly on them. The factors can be given a tentative label if some particular variables or set of variables "load" strongly on them. For example, our first factor, which accounts for a third of total variance is clearly a joint marital factor as it is strongly correlated with husband's and wife's t.a.e. and class prestige value. T.a.e. and class are very closely connected as the analysis has been unable to separate them. But t.a.e is clearly a more important component than class. One might regard this as the skill or talent or intellectual aspect of class and I have labelled it "joint occupational competence". The next important factor is clearly also a joint factor, but by contrast it loads heavily on age at marriage and on hardly anything else, showing clearly the linear independence of assortative mating for age from other variables which we suspected from earlier analysis. Other factors relate to one or the other spouse only rather than to both, such as sibship size, and mobility. Some variables (class, population) are strongly influenced by several factors, some of which are joint, others are not.

Of course these patterns will depend on the variables which are collected and included in the sample, but I think they give a good idea of the relative strength of association between husbands and wives. I hope that more able statisticians than I will be able to develop this sort of approach and sociologists will become more interested in interpreting this sort of data. No statistical analysis can tell which of these correlates are the result of conscious choice and which are reflections of similarity of social or geographical background, which were necessary but not sufficient, to bring the couple together. Only judgment based on a better knowledge of human behaviour can tell us that.

The Broader Context of Assortative Mating

CHOICE, ASSORTATIVE MATING AND ARRANGED MARRIAGES

Assortative mating, in its interesting sense, clearly depends on some kind of choice being available to each partner or being made on his or her behalf. But in many societies, both simple and complex, the scope of marriage partner is rigorously defined and restricted by custom and in some cases the marriage is arranged, with little thought to the preferences of the partners themselves. Depending on the customs, this may influence the similarity between the partners in comparison with the consequences of their own choice or of a random choice. The primacy of need for a suitable match on caste, class or dynastic grounds may reduce correlations for conventionally measured traits to a low level or to complete insignificance, on the supposition that like will tend to choose like. And the similarity between the spouses may be no more than that between any pair picked at random from their own endogamous subset in contrast to the rest of the population.

An example of an advanced culture where arranged marriages are, or were, very common is Japan. Traditionally marriages there are arranged between families by a "nakohdo" or go-between (Vogel, 1961). In Japan the assortative mating for height, which always shows a positive correlation in surveys in the West, seems to be almost non-existent (Furusho, 1961), although there is some evidence for variation in skin colour by class, for which assortative mating might be inferred (Hulse, 1967).

In societies structured by caste some assortative mating might be expected anyway through the general relatedness of the endogamous group, if representatives of the whole populations are included in the sample. In Sikh populations married in India but living in Britain there is certainly assortative mating for skin colour (Roberts and Kahlon, 1972) to the extent of a correlation of 0·349 (max.) for forehead skin reflectance.

A number of studies of simple societies have failed to reveal any obvious assortative mating at all. Data published by Spuhler on the Ramah Navaho, for example, on 40 anthropometric measurements, are as often negative as positive and none attain any level of statistical significance. In this population size (619) the choice of mates available to any individual would have been very small (Spuhler, 1968).

One well known example of restricted choice is rules governing the exogamous marital sections of some Australian aborigines (Yengoyan, 1968). If the rules are kept there may be an average choice of 6–12 mates, in a good year. Some suggest that the rules are not always kept— indeed that it is impossible for the rules to be kept and that this is recognized by the actors.

These considerations apply to biological characteristics. Opposite conclusions might well be drawn for socially measured characters such as class or income. Especially where marriages are traditionally arranged it seems very likely that the similarity between the income, class, political affiliation of the spouses or at least of their families will be much higher than the similarity which would follow from the partner's natural choice, and by contrast the level of psychological or physical similarity may be less.

ASSORTATIVE AND DISASSORTATIVE MATING FOR CLASS AND GEOGRAPHICAL ORIGIN, AND GENETICAL RELATEDNESS

An interesting attempt to integrate the genetical consequences of social choice has been made by Harrison and his colleagues in their study of Otmoor and Oxford City. The problem to be solved is the way in which assortative or disassortative marriage in relation to class and to geographical origins might affect the social and geographical distribution of socially invisible genes which may be assumed to be present at different frequencies in the primary classes and geographical areas (Harrison et al., 1970).

The initial assumption is that none of the classes or areas have any genotypic relatedness, that is, they do not share any common ancestry. The patterns of exchange between classes by intergenerational movement and by marriage, and between areas by marital movement, from 1837 to 1967 were incorporated into an exchange matrix. This model was iterated to see how many generations elapsed for a given increase in relatedness. After sixteen generations or about 500 years the effects of intergenerational social mobility alone had increased relatedness—that is the percentage of ancestors which each group had in common with the other—to an average of 95 per cent. Twenty generations elapsed before the effects of marital exchange, measured separately, had such an homogenizing effect on relatedness. In both cases the pattern is for the manual group to become homogeneous after a few generations, the non-manual "middle" classes also coalesce into a single group and several more generations are needed to bring these two groups into a level of 95 per cent relatedness with each other. This is very much in accord with what is known about the segregation of marriage markets among the middle and working class in Britain at the present day (Hope, 1972). This study is, of course, about the consequences of disassortative mating (i.e. class exchanges) on genetic markers for which assortative mating, indeed any choice at all, should be impossible. Assortative mating would tend to conserve low levels of relatedness but it has to be almost absolute to have effect on socially invisible genes. By contrast, genes for characters important in mate selection can be expected to have their heterogeneous distributions preserved or even enhanced, according to the models of Young and Gibson (1963). In Oxford City in marriages of the same period a rather more rapid homogenization of ancestry was achieved. The barriers of marriage between the classes and to intergenerational mobility were stronger in the country. But Hiorns and his colleagues point out (Hiorns et al., 1973) that although this leads to more rapid homogeneity for socially invisible genes in the town, the social classes might become correspondingly more heterogeneous for those genes which may be involved in mate selection and in social promotion.

Conclusion

An attempt to discuss assortative mating on the British marital scene is made difficult by the poverty of data especially with respect to social and psychological studies. Most work which is quoted is based on studies in the USA and it is difficult to know how far the United States experience is applicable here. In this context I suspect that the relative role of "propinquity" in relation to "homogamy" may be rather less here in the UK than it is alleged to be in the United States.

The results summarized in this paper show that in general, assortative mating is strong for social variables, relatively weak for physical variables and may be either for psychological ones. The theoretical development of the study of these sets of variables is also at rather different levels. The genetical consequences of assortative mating for biological characters have attracted a lot of attention and a body of detailed theory exists to account for them. Especially for physical characters which are unambiguously measurable and have a high heritability, clear prediction can readily be made. The causes of biological assortative mating have been largely ignored by biologists. They are usually assumed to be non-biological, but this problem has also been largely ignored by sociologists and psychologists. Assortative mating for social and psychological characters, by contrast, have attracted a lot of research to gather empirical fact and also to propose theories on causation, but no organized body of theory seems to exist on the consequences of assortative mating for social characters, despite its apparent potential for widening and preserving differences in society.

Lastly the genetic aspects of assortative mating—or disassortative mating—raise some interesting social questions. Enough class intermarriage seems to exist in some British populations to destroy any heterogeneity by class which may exist for socially invisible genetic markers. But insofar as disassortative mating for class is accelerated by the pre-eminence of strong assortative mating for ability, then the rapid elimination of socially unimportant genetical differences may necessarily be accompanied by the preservation or accentuation of socially prominent genetical differences. But this area of study is still *terra incognita* to many students of social questions, and possibly also *terra incommoda*.

Acknowledgements

I am grateful to the SSRC for a grant in connection with the Reading Marriage Survey and to Professor D. V. Glass for help with the P.I.C. survey analysis.

References

Beckman, L. (1962). Assortative mating in man. *Eugenics Review*, **54**, 63–67.

Beckman, L. and Elston, R. (1962). Assortative mating and fertility. *Acta Genetica et Statistica Medica* (Basel), **12**, 117–122.

Berent, J. (1954). Social mobility and marriage: a study of trends in England and Wales. In *Social Mobility in Britain*. Edited by D. V. Glass. London: Routledge and Kegan Paul.

Bossard, J. H. S. (1932). Residential propinquity as a factor in marriage selection. *American Journal of Sociology*, **38**, 219–224.

Bowerman, C. E. and Day, B. R. (1956). A test of the theory of complementary needs as applied to couples during courtship. *American Sociological Review*, **21**, 602–605.

Burgess, E. W. and Wallin, P. (1943). Homogamy in social characteristics. *American Journal of Sociology*, **49**, 109–124.

Burt, C. and Howard, M. (1956). The multifactorial theory of inheritance and its application to intelligence. *British Journal of Statistical Psychology*, **9**, 95–131.

Butler, D. and Stokes, D. (1969). *Political Change in Britain*. London: Macmillan.

Canter, S. (1969). Personality traits in twins (unpublished). Cited in *The Study of Twins*. P. Mittler (1971). Harmondsworth, Middx.: Penguin Books.

Catton, W. R. and Smircich, R. J. (1964). Mathematical models for residential propinquity and mate selection. *American Sociological Review*, **29**, 522–529.

Coleman, D. A. (1973). Marriage movement in British cities. In *Genetic Variation in Britain*. Edited by D. F. Roberts and E. Sunderland. London: Taylor and Francis.

Crow, J. F. and Felsenstein, J. (1968). The effects of assortative mating on the genetic composition of a population. *Eugenics Quarterly*, **15**, 85–97.

Erlenmeyer-Kimling, L. and Jarvik, L. F. (1963). Genetics and intelligence: a review. *Science*, **142**, 1477–1479.

Furusho, T. (1961). Genetic study on stature. *Japanese Journal of Human Genetics*, **6**, 78–101.

Galton, F. (1883). *Inquiry into Human Faculty and its Development*. London: Macmillan.

Gibson, J. B. and Mascie-Taylor, C. G. N. (1973). Biological aspects of a high socio-economic group. II. I.Q. components and social mobility. *Journal of Biosocial Science*, **5**, 17–30.

Girard, A. (1964). *Le Choix du Conjoint*. Paris: I.N.E.D.

Glass, D. V. (Editor) (1954). *Social Mobility in Britain*. London: Routledge and Kegan Paul.

Glass, D. V. (1976). Recent and prospective trends in fertility in developed countries. *Philosophical Transactions of the Royal Society* B, **274**, 1–52.

Godfrey, J. (1958). Social behaviour in four bank vole races. *Animal Behaviour*, **6**, 117.

Goldthorpe, J. H. and Hope, K. (1974). *The Social Grading of Occupations*. Oxford: Clarendon.

Griffiths, R. W. and Kunz, P. R. (1973). Assortative mating: a study of physiognomic homogamy. *Social Biology*, **20**, 448–453.

Hall, J. and Jones, D. Caradog (1950). The social grading of occupations. *British Journal of Sociology*, **1**, 31–55.

Harrison, G. A., Gibson, J. B. and Hiorns, R. W. (1976). Assortative marriage for psychometric, personality and anthropometric variations in a group of Oxfordshire villages. *Journal of Biosocial Science*, **8**, 145–153.

Harrison, G. A., Hiorns, R. W. and Küchemann, C. F. (1970). Social class relatedness in some Oxfordshire villages. *Journal of Biosocial Science*, **2**, 71–80.

Hiorns, R. W., Harrison, G. A. and Küchemann, C. F. (1973). Factors affecting the genetical structure of populations: an urban-rural contrast in Britain. In *Genetic Variation in Britain*. Edited by D. F. Roberts and E. Sunderland. London: Taylor and Francis.

Hope, K. (1972). Marriage markets in the stratification system. In *The Analysis of Social Mobility. Methods and Approaches*. Edited by K. Hope. Oxford: Clarendon Press.

Hulse, F. S. (1967). Selection for skin colour among Japanese. *American Journal of Physical Anthropology*, **27**, 143–155.

Jacobsohn, P. and Matheny, A. P. (1963). Mate selection in open marriage systems. In *International Studies in Sociology and Social Anthropology*, Vol. 1. *Family and Marriage*. Leiden: E. J. Brill.

Jensen, A. R. (1969). How much can we boost IQ and scholastic achievement? *Harvard Educational Review*, **39**, 1–123.

Kennedy, R. J. (1943). Premarital residential propinquity rnd ethnic endogamy. *American Journal of Sociology*. **48**, 50–64.

Kerckhoff, A. C. (1963). Patterns of homogamy and the field of eligibles. *Social Forces*, **42**, 289–297.

Kerckhoff, A. C. and Davis, K. E. (1962). Value consensus and need complementarity in mate selection. *American Sociological Review*, **27**, 295–303.

Kilham, P. and Klopfer, P. H. (1968). The construct race and the innate differential. In *Science and the Concept of Race*. Edited by M. Mead, Th. Dobzhansky, E. Tobach and R. E. Light. New York: Columbia University Press.

Knight, G. R., Robertson, A. and Waddington, C. H. (1956). Selection for sexual isolation within a species. *Evolution*, **10**, 14–22.

Lill, A. (1968). An analysis of sexual isolation in the domestic fowl: 1. The basis of homogamy in males; 2. The basis of homogamy in females. *Behaviour*, **30**, 107–145.

Maslow, A. (1955). Deficiency motivation and growth motivation. In *Current Theory and Research in Motivation*. Nebraska: Nebraska University Press.

Nias, D. (1975). *Personality and Other Factors Determining the Recreational Interests of Children and Adults*. University of London Ph.D. Thesis.

Pearson, K. and others (1903). Assortative mating in man. *Biometrika*, **2**, 481–498.

Pearson, K. and Lee, A. (1903). On the laws of inheritance in man: 1. Inheritance of physical characters. *Biometrika*, **2**, 357–462.

Penrose, L. S. (1944). Mental illness in husband and wife: a contribution to the study of assortative mating in man. *Psychiatric Quarterly Supplement*, **18**, 161.

Pierce, R. M. (1963). Marriage in the fifties. *Sociological Review*, **11**, 215–240.

Pomerat, C. M. (1936). Homogamy and infertility. *Human Biology*, **8**, 19–24.

Roberts, D. F. and Kahlon, D. P. S. (1972). Skin pigmentation and assortative mating in Sikhs. *Journal of Biosocial Science*, **4**, 91–100.

Rose, R. (1976). *The Problems of Party Government*. Harmondsworth, Middx.: Penguin Books.

Shields, J. (1962). *Monozygotic Twins Brought up Apart and Brought up Together*. London and New York: Oxford University Press.

Sindberg, R. M., Roberts, A. F. and McClain, D. (1972). Mate selection factors in computer matched marriages. *Journal of Marriage and the Family*, **34**, 611–614.

Spuhler, J. N. (1968). Assortative mating with respect to physical characteristics. *Eugenics Quarterly*, **15**, 128–140.

Susanne, C. (1967). Contributions a l'étude de l'assortiment matrimonial dans un échantillon de la population Belge. *Bullétin de la Société Royale Belge d'Anthropologie et de Préhistoire*, **78**, 147–196.

Susanne, C. (1975). Analyse multivariée dans une étude de l'assortiment matrimonial. *Homo*, **25**, 166–171.

Taeuber, I. B. (1934). *Assortative Mating for Colour in the American Negro*. Third International Congress of Eugenics, 1932. Baltimore: Williams and Wilkins.

Tanner, J. M. (1962). *Growth at Adolescence*. Oxford: Blackwell Scientific Press.

Thoday, J. M. (1964). Genetics and the integration of reproductive systems. *Symposia of the Royal Entomological Society of London*, **2**, 108–119.

Tomici, L. (1939). Fattori somatici dell'attrazione matrimoniale nei coniugi sassaresi. *Genus*. **4**, 1–36.

Vogel, E. (1961). The go-between in a developing society: the case of the Japanese marriage arranger. *Human Organisation*, **20**, 112–120.

Warren, B. L. (1966). A multiple variable approach to the assortative mating phenomenon. *Eugenics Quarterly*, **13**, 285–290.

Willoughby, R. R. (1933). Somatic homogamy in man. *Human Biology*, **5**, 690–705.

Wilson, G. and Nias, D. (1976). *Love's Mysteries*. London: Open Books.

Winch, R. F. (1955). The theory of complementary needs in mate selection: final results on the test of the general hypothesis. *American Sociological Review*, **20**, 552–555.

Winch, R. F. (1967). Another look at the theory of complementary needs in mate selection. *Journal of Marriage and the Family*, **29**, 756–762.

Winch, R. F., Ktsanes, T. and Ktsanes, V. (1954). The theory of complementary needs in mate selection: an analytic and descriptive study. *American Sociological Review*, **19**, 241–249.

Woodside, M. (1946). Courtship and mating in an urban community. *Eugenics Review*. **XXXVIII**, 29–39.

Yengoyan, A. A. (1968). Demographic and ecological influences on aboriginal Australian marriage sections. In *Man the Hunter*. Edited by R. Lee and I. DeVore. Chicago and New York: Aldine/Atherton.

Young, M. and Gibson, J. (1963). In search of an explanation of social mobility. *British Journal of Statistical Psychology*. **XVI**, 27–35.

Zipf, G. K. (1949). *Human Behaviour and the Principle of Least Effort: An Introduction to Human Ecology*. Cambridge, Massachusetts: Addison Wesley.

Youthful Marriage:
The Vortex of Disadvantage

BERNARD INEICHEN

Department of Sociology, University of Bristol, Bristol, England

Teenage marriage has been until very recently rising steadily in popularity, as part of the general decline in the age of marriage, in Britain and in other industrialized countries. In the early 1920s only 8 per cent of brides marrying in England and Wales were aged under 20. By 1970, this figure had reached 31 per cent. Only 9 per cent of women born in 1930 married as teenagers but among women born a quarter of a century later, in 1955, the figure had more than doubled to 19 per cent.

There are signs recently of a reversal in this trend (see Leete, 1976 and Leete's contribution to this volume). Yet it is undoubtedly true that a high rate of early marriage still persists. While there is speculation and argument about the causes of this trend, what I want to consider in this paper are the circumstances of those who enter marriage at a comparatively youthful age. What has been established is that such couples tend to lack occupational skills, and to produce their first child relatively rapidly.

One of those who has looked at this group is Griselda Rowntree (1962; 1964). In the first issue of *New Society*, (4th October 1962), she contributed an article entitled "New Facts on Teenage Marriage" which described a sample of 500 brides marrying in the 1950s of whom nearly one-third were teenagers. Although the teenage brides were shown to have been significantly more likely than older brides to have had fathers in social class V, to have had a manual job themselves, to have married a husband himself in his teens, to have had a child early in marriage and to have failed to have achieved an independent home, the author was sanguine about the outcome of such marriages, in contrast to the wartime marriages of the previous decade. She felt able to conclude:

> It may well be that there are today even better prospects for success in teenage marriage than there have been in the recent past.

The evidence available does not however give substance to that pious hope. In a later article (Rowntree, 1964) she reports over 20 per cent of teenage wives who had experienced parting from their husbands (whether or not this led to divorce), against a figure of 8½ per cent for the whole sample.

TABLE I
Proportion of teenage brides separating

	N=	Percentage parting (at some time separated from spouse, whether or not this led to divorce)	Percentage contemplating separation (but did not actually part)
All couples	1340	8·5	3·8
Teenage brides only	181	21·1	6·1
Teenage brides: infertile	23	56·0	8·7
fertile before marriage	50	26·0	8·0
fertile after marriage	108	11·1	4·6

Adapted from Rowntree (1964).

The work on divorce by Colin Gibson indicates that among a sample divorcing in 1961, couples who had married when both were teenagers were three times as likely to end in the divorce court as marriages where both partners were older. When only the wife was a teenager the rate was still twice the normal divorce rate (Gibson, 1974, 1975). A similar association of youthful age at marriage and a high divorce rate has been reported from American studies. (Monahan, 1953; Glick, 1957; Lowrie, 1965; Burchinal, 1965; Bumpass and Sweet, 1972). Moss (1965) quotes evidence of a similar association from Sweden.

Some have suggested that youthful marriages contain a proportion which are entered into in order to escape from an unhappy domestic situation (Moss and Gingles, 1959; Rochefort, 1961; Dominian, 1968). Such marriages are likely to be particularly vulnerable, in that the personalities of these couples may be immature and, therefore, the least suitable to embark on early marriage. Everyday observation suggests there is some truth in this, although the numbers are likely to be quite small as a percentage of all first marriages. One per cent of Rowntree's 1964 sample, for instance, comprises teenage wives whose infertile marriages had already broken up. A further one per cent is comprised of similar wives in their early twenties.

The picture of youthful marriage overall is rather more complex. It is dominated above all by the influence of social class and early pregnancy.

Teenage marriage has been shown to be twice as common among semi-skilled and unskilled workers than among non-manual husbands in two large studies (Pierce, 1963; Peel and Carr, 1975). In 1960/1, about 80 per cent of teenage brides had manual worker husbands. Gibson (1974) notes that:

> the trend towards earlier marriage is mainly due to the increasing tendency of working-class brides to marry before the age of 20.

Similar evidence is again available from America (Burchinal, 1965; Moss, 1965).

In many cases these marriages are precipitated by pregnancy. The Registrar General's figures indicate that one-third of the teenage brides marrying in 1969/70 were pregnant, compared with 16 per cent of brides aged 20–24, and 43 per cent of all births conceived premaritally were to teenage mothers. More of Rowntree's sample of teenage brides had had a child by the time they were interviewed, 81·8 per cent compared with 72·5 per cent of wives who had married at a later age. In the large sample investigated by Woolf (1971) the mean period between marriage and the birth of the first child was 1·7 years for teenage brides, against 2·4 years for older brides. In the recent study by Peel and Carr (1975) two-thirds of those conceiving before marriage were teenagers, against just over one-quarter of those not pregnant in the first year or so of marriage.

These young mothers come predominantly from the lower occupational classes. Work in Aberdeen (Baird and Illsley, 1953; Gill et al., 1970; see also Newson and Newson, 1963; Lowrie, 1965) shows a pattern of youthful mothers more common in lower social classes. A sample taken over a number of years showed, for example, that 29 per cent of legitimate first pregnancies to class IV–V mothers were to teenagers. For the wives in professional and clerical jobs the figure was 12 per cent.

Youthful marriage and low occupational status together make a poor prognosis for the success of a marriage. Gibson (1974, 1975) notes the association of a high divorce rate with low social class and points out the steady rise in the percentage of young brides among divorcing couples as one descends the occupational class scale (see Table II).

TABLE II

Proportion of divorcing wives in each social class who married under the age of (a) 20 and (b) 25 years of age, by husband's social class at marriage

	Husband's social class at marriage					
---	I–II	III Nm	III	IV	V	All
Age of wives at marriage (percentage)						
Under 20	19	18	33	41	45	32
Under 25	58	73	82	72	85	76

Adapted from Gibson (1974).

Gibson also notes the association of premarital pregnancy with a high rate of divorce and a similar finding is reported from America (Bumpass and Sweet, 1972).

I would now like to turn to my own work in Bristol with a sample of nearly 200 newly-married couples. These couples have been interviewed two or three times during the first 18 months of their married life.* Interviews have concentrated on their housing situation, which was recognized by Pierce's sample as the most frequently reported problem area for those marrying in the 1950s (Pierce, 1963).

In many respects the Bristol couples confirm the picture of relative deprivation in youthful marriage described by Rowntree. They received validation more recently on a national basis from the work of Peel and Carr (1975) which, while focussing on a different aspect of family life, confirms the overall picture of the association of youthful marriage with low occupational class and rapid fertility.

The Bristol couples cannot, because of the brevity of the research, tell us much directly about divorce rates but they do provide material which illustrates the vulnerability towards divorce of lower-class couples described by Gibson (1974, 1975).

I think that my sample was reasonably representative of all young couples (the age limit was 35) marrying for the first time in Bristol in early

---

* An earlier study of the housing circumstances of a smaller group of couples has been completed (Ineichen 1975a). Both samples were combined in a subsequent paper (Ineichen 1975b) using material from the first interview only. Other papers, including one on housing and fertility, are in preparation.

1974. Of the 179 brides, 68 (37 per cent) were teenagers. 19 (11 per cent) were really young, marrying at the age of 16 or 17. Teenage husbands were much rarer for it was found that only fourteen of the teenage brides, plus three older brides, married husbands in their teens.

The teenage brides were more likely than older brides to have a husband in semi-skilled or unskilled manual work and they were more likely to have a manual job themselves. Teenage marriage is likely to be a working-class event. Of the 68 teenage brides, 58 married husbands in manual jobs and nearly one-third of the teenagers were in manual work themselves. Most brides in manual work, in fact, married as teenagers. Details are given in Table III.

TABLE III
Teenage and older brides

	Teenage	Older
	brides	brides
N=	68	111
Percentage with teenage grooms	19	4
Percentage with grooms in		
(i) non-manual job	15	45
(ii) skilled manual job	48	38
(iii) semi-skilled or unskilled job	37	17
Percentage in manual work themselves	29	14

The same proportion of teenage and older brides had fathers in class IV or V jobs (19 per cent from each age-group). Rather more of the teenage brides came from council-house backgrounds (62 per cent against 49 per cent) and, as Table IV shows, the younger brides (and to a lesser extent, their grooms) come from larger families of origin.

TABLE IV

	Number of siblings (mean)	
	Teenage brides	Older brides
Brides	2·6	1·7
Grooms	2·7	2·3

When one looks at the courtship pattern of teenage brides, this is of briefer duration than for older brides (see Table V); and teenage brides, as other workers have found out, become pregnant much more quickly. Table VI gives the details.

TABLE V
Length of time known before marriage (percentages)

	Teenage brides	Older brides
Acquainted under three years	62	42
Acquainted three years or longer	32	48
No information	6	9
Engaged under eleven months	57	36
Engaged eleven months or more	37	52
No information	6	12

The chances of a teenage bride being pregnant is four times that of an older bride, for this sample.

TABLE VI
Fertility (percentages)

	Teenage brides	Older brides
Pregnant at marriage	40	10
At interview		
Known to be pregnant or had child already	37	12
Expected to have child within 2 years	24	26
Expected to have child after over 2 years	36	53
Did not intend to have children	1	5
No information	1	4

There is an association for the whole sample between premarital conception and low social class: 18 of the 44 (41 per cent) in the two lowest classes were pregnant at marriage, compared with 5 out of 58 (9 per cent) of the brides of non-manual husbands. Looking just at the teenage brides, there is an even stronger association between premarital pregnancy and occupational class. One in ten of the wives of non-manual husbands, one in three of the wives of skilled workers, and three in five of the wives of semi-skilled or unskilled workers were pregnant at marriage.

Future expectations concerning family size (asked at the first interview) indicate that it will be some time before this differential is eliminated. A majority of the teenage brides were either pregnant already or expected to have a child within 2 years of marriage and this included all but two of the 19 brides aged under 18. By the time the survey was completed, 18 months after marriage, almost one-half of the teenage brides (33 out of 68) were pregnant or had had a child, compared with 29 of the 111 (26 per cent) of older brides.

The eventual anticipated family size of the two groups (based on answers given at the first interview) is however very similar. Details are given in Table VII.

TABLE VII
Eventual family size (percentages)

	Teenage brides	Older brides
Two children or less	9	12
Two children	53	49
Two children or more	19	20
Three children or more	12	7
No information	7	12

The relative occupational disadvantage of the younger brides and their grooms (see Table III) is compounded rapidly by their loss of earning abilities. It is the wives of the husbands who lack occupational skills who are particularly prone to loss of earnings. One-half of the teenage wives of class IV and V husbands were earning nothing at interview, against 30 per cent of the class III teenage wives and 20 per cent of the non-manual teenage wives: only one-quarter were earning over £20 per week, against almost half of the teenage wives of more skilled husbands.

The relatively weak financial situation of the teenage wives is reflected by their inferior housing situation. Just over one-half of them (against just under one-quarter of the older wives) started married life with relatives. More than twice as many had, by the time of our first interview, unsuccessfully sought to enter the privately rented market. In fact, the experience was common to one-third of our teenage brides. One-half, at first interview, had savings of less than £100 but only about 30 per cent of the older wives had failed to reach this figure.

In the course of the study, the number of teenage brides becoming owner-occupiers (35 per cent) was almost matched by those becoming council tenants (28 per cent). Among older brides, the difference was considerable: 56 per cent owner-occupiers against 7 per cent council tenants.

Taking into account expectations expressed at the end of the study, after couples had been married for 18 months, the figure for future owner-occupation would probably reach 46 per cent among teenage brides, and 76 per cent among older ones; for council tenants the likely figures were 37 per cent and 14 per cent.

A further interesting comparison is to look at the jobs done by the wives at marriage and the age at marriage. Separating out the wives who were in manual jobs, the majority of these (20 out of 35) married as teenagers. These younger manual wives are more likely to be married to a husband in a lower occupational class and to be aiming for a council tenancy. Table VIII gives the details. The number of older manual brides who are heading for owner-occupations is particularly striking.

TABLE VIII
Brides in manual work

	Teenage manual brides	Older manual brides
Percentage of brides in manual jobs who (i) have husbands in occupational class		
I–II	5	27
III Nm	5	0
III	50	53
IV	20	20
V	20	0
(ii) have probable final housing outcome		
owner-occupation	35	80
council tenant	60	20
undecided	5	0
N=	20	15

Put in another fashion, some of these results could be expressed as follows.

1. Most of the brides marrying class IV or V husbands are teenagers.
2. Most of the brides in manual jobs are teenagers.
3. Most of the brides who are sharing homes after marriage are teenagers.
4. Most of the husbands in the lowest income bracket (under £25 per week) have married teenagers.
5. Most of the pregnant brides are teenagers.
6. Most of the brides who gave up paid work soon after marriage are teenagers.

7. Most of the brides who go into council tenancies are teenagers.
8. About one wife in ten in the whole sample is a teenager, with a husband in semi-skilled or unskilled work, starting married life with relatives.

Although the survey covered only the first 18 months of married life, ten couples have experienced separations. In three instances this was due solely to the inability to find somewhere to live, and these couples were now together again. Two other couples had split up for a time but now were together again. Five had apparently separated for good. Of these ten couples five brides had married as teenagers, the other five were aged 21, and the husband of one was a teenager.

Overcrowding was more common among teenage brides. 14 of the sharing couples were severely overcrowded at the start of their married life. (4 were in two-bedroomed houses with at least 3 other people; 9 in three-bedroomed houses with at least 4 other people; and one in a four-bedroomed house with 7 other people: 8 of the brides were pregnant).

Of these 14 brides (including seven of the pregnant ones) 11 married as teenagers. The *average* age of this group of overcrowded brides was just over 18 years.

The pattern for teenage marriage, when contrasted with the marriages of older brides, therefore seems to be:

1. Early pregnancy, often as a result of premarital conception.
2. Material disadvantage: relatively low status jobs, plus low earnings after marriage, combining with difficulties over housing; the eventual prospect of a council tenancy rather than owner-occupation.
3. An eventual higher rate of divorce (with concomitant housing problems both before *and* after); and possibly greater vulnerability to other forms of social pathology such as homelessness and child abuse.

It is worth considering each of these stages in turn. I would like to do this by posing, and attempting to answer, three questions.

1. Why does there continue to be, given the relatively easy availability of acceptable techniques of birth control, such a high rate of pregnancy among teenage brides?
2. What happens in the early years of marriage to those who married young? What decisions are they faced with, and how are these decision taken?
3. Do such marriages show high rates of various kinds of pathology, and if so, do we know why?

These questions are obviously to some extent inter-related.

Firstly, the high rates of premarital pregnancies. The relatively lax sexual codes concerning premarital intercourse within one setting of the culture of poverty have been described by Lee Rainwater. Within the notorious (and now largely demolished) black ghetto of Pruitt-Igoe in St Louis over half the girls had their first pregnancy by the time they were 18 (Rainwater, 1971). Pregnancy is assumed to the *girl's* mistake, and the view that "everyone is entitled to one mistake" is commonly held. There is "an implicit assumption that (girls) have no right to their virginity".

Other studies of contraceptive practice in America and Britain have confirmed a picture of low usage among young people persisting up to and beyond the introduction of the contraceptive pill. Of the young people interviewed in Britain by Michael Schofield's study of sexual behaviour, for example, less than one-third of those sexually experienced at 18 had always used contraceptives; almost one-half had never used any form of birth control. Of the sexually experienced girls 61 per cent said they never took precautions, and only 35 per cent insisted that their partners did. Seven years later, at the age of 25, a staggering 24 per cent were sexually experienced but had hardly ever, or never, used any kind of contraceptive method (Schofield, 1973).

In a study of over 300 couples marrying in Hull in 1965/6 (of whom about 20 per cent were pregnant at marriage) only just over one-half (53 per cent) had used contraception before the first pregnancy (Peel, 1972).

Investigations of older samples (Rainwater, 1960; Land, 1969; Askham, 1975) confirm that many parents of large families seldom get around to using any form of birth control until their family has reached the maximum tolerable size, which is quite late in a couple's sexual career. Early married life between such couples is likely to be marked by poor communication between the spouses (poor communication about sex is one part of this) and by a generally fatalistic attitude to life. As Chamberlain (1976) has pointed out, a fatalistic attitude to contraception is part of this.

Recent research suggests that large families may become very rare indeed: only 1·1 per cent of the wives interviewed by Peel and Carr (1975) expressed a wish for more than four children. Yet a class difference does remain in the use of contraceptives. Couples where the husband's job is semi-skilled or unskilled manual, or the wife's is manual, do show a rather lower rate of use (Peel and Carr, 1975).

This class difference is also probably true of my sample of newly-married couples in Bristol, and for explanation we must go beyond the merely physiological. There are very positive social reasons why young working-class girls should want to have babies, which outweigh pressures towards the use of contraceptives. Here are some.

1. It gets them out of dead-end jobs. For these girls there is little of the problem of the typical readers of the women's page of the *Guardian* which is a heart-searching conflict between a family or a career.

2. It bestows adult status. To quote Gibson (1975):

> Unsuccessful in a society which applauds the virtue of higher education, working-class girls graduate to the one role that is acclaimed by the gramophone records they hear, the magazines they read and the television they view. For them marriage and motherhood is a clear expression of success in a role and function which, however feminists may regret it, is still seen by most women as their ultimate goal in most working-class communities of today. The wedding ring, pram and double bed are the young wives primary marks of achievement over their still unmarried middle-class sisters of similar age.

3. Working-class value systems endorse the raising of a family and mark out as deviant (possibly selfish and even unnatural) those who do not marry and have children.

4. In view of (3) above, an argument can be made for "having children" and "having them when you are young". After all, the "right" time for having children is fairly closely defined.

> . . . a 'girl' of twenty will be considered by most people to be too young to be tied down by the cares of looking after a family, whereas a married woman of 26 or 27 is thought to be leaving it rather late if she intends to have a family at all. In addition, the evidence indicates that a large proportion of marriages under the age of 20 are precipitated by the girl becoming pregnant; while experience suggests that once a woman has reached 26 or so, a strong motivation factor may be the fear of being left on the shelf. (Newson and Newson, 1963).

Further, once begun, the pressures to go on with family building are considerable. Only children, says popular wisdom, are brought up "spoiled" and "lonely". "If you are going to have children therefore, and have them while you are young, you might as well have them close together".

The other side of the coin to this is resistance to the idea of abortion. As well as the idea of fatalism, summed up in the expression "I fell for a baby", there are puritan values of retribution for illicit enjoyment: "I've had my pleasure and now I must pay for it".

These suggestions are frankly speculative—yet fewer than 10 per cent of the teenage girls interviewed by Schofield said thay would consider an abortion if they conceived outside marriage (Schofield, 1973). More recently published work again shows a class gradient in attitudes to abortion among recently-married women, with the same groups that were relatively resistant to contraception, also resistant to abortion (Peel and Carr, 1975).

Finally, there are the workings of the housing market. If you feel that your destiny is to be a council tenant (and this may be the only way to get a home of your own) the longer you remain infertile the longer you will take to achieve your goal.

Once you are in the council sector, this process may continue. The only way to get yourself, your husband and your toddler out of the flat on the fourteenth floor (short of jumping) is to have another child as quickly as possible, ideally of the opposite sex to the first.

This last point has led me into the next subject I want to discuss: the kind of decisions young couples face in early marriage.

When marriage begins with an extended period of childlessness, the wife will continue in employment, and the marriage is likely to be marked by relative egalitarianism and sharing. But such an experience is comparatively unlikely among the youngest couples who rapidly enter parenthood. This is especially true, as we have seen, of the young working-class married couples.

As Alice Rossi (1968) puts it:

When pregnancy was likely to follow shortly after marriage, the major transition point in a woman's life is marriage itself. This transition is increasingly the first pregnancy rather than marriage.

The birth of a child makes egalitarianism much more difficult to attain. The experience of young working-class couples is such that:

1. They have had a very short time to get to know one another.
2. They have very little experience of life on which to build.
3. They have little opportunity to develop their own style of intimacy as so many of them start their married life with parents. The difficulties of sharing are widely acknowledged (Inselberg, 1962). Getting a home of their own is a desired goal, yet it also can create problems of its own. One wife liked her first home, a flat in a high-rise block, and was reasonably happy living there with her husband and her baby. The husband, though, preferred it when they had been staying with her mother. There he could go out with his mates when he chose; now he had to stay in in the evenings, or his wife complained of feeling lonely!

Finally, there are the financial pressures, again usually the result of the arrival of a child rather than youthful marriage itself. One income has to feed three, instead of two incomes feeding two. The husband may give up a "job with a future" to take something that pays better in the short run. And the wife may have to prove herself with the establishment of an independent home, simultaneously in her new roles as housewife and mother. Confirmation of the lasting economic disadvantage faced by those who marry and have children while young comes from a study of over a thousand couples in Detroit (Freedman and Coombs, 1966).

The third question I have raised concerns the levels of pathology in youthful marriages. It is well established that youthful marriages are particularly prone to divorce. What can we say about the cause of this association? And are such marriages also particularly vulnerable to other kinds of pathology?

The evidence I shall consider is fragmentary but at times alarming. One study, Anthony Ryle's *Neurosis in the Ordinary Family*, (1967), finds no association between the quality of marriage (assessed by an interviewer) and age at marriage, in a sample of 100 working-class couples. Indeed, those who married younger are assessed as having marginally happier marriages, although the difference is not significant. An earlier study of English working-class marriages (Slater and Woodside, 1951) had similarly failed to find an association between age at marriage and happiness of marriage.

However, two studies of baby battering yield rather alarming results. The average age of the mothers of a sample of 134 battered children investigated by a team in Birmingham was 19·7 years, four years younger than the national average age for mothers at the birth of their first child, and one-third of the mothers were unmarried. Three-quarters of the parents were from social class IV and V (Smith, 1975).

Another study, of 34 battered children in Wiltshire, found the mean age of mother at marriage or cohabitation to be 21. Again 24 of the 34 fathers were unskilled labourers (Oliver *et al.*, 1974).

Another social problem in which the participants display surprising youthfulness is homelessness. Over one-quarter of the women given the status of homeless in the London sample studied by Greve *et al.*, (1971) between 1966 and 1969 were under 25. Among those applying for temporary accommodation on the grounds of homelessness for one four-week period in 1969, no fewer than 9 per cent were teenage wives. Nearly one-half of these families had never had a home of their own. "Homelessness for these families was usually the result of disputes with relatives, overcrowding, or landlord pressure" (Greve *et al.*, 1971). Their small size as families meant that alternative accommodation could be found for them more easily—explaining in part why they did not figure so largely in actual admissions into temporary accommodation. Among London-born women in the sample, youth is especially apparent: nearly half are under 25, and 15 per cent teenagers (Greve *et al.*, 1971).

Another study conducted at the same time in the West Country reported as follows:

> Young families are particularly vulnerable to the risk of homelessness. At the time of entering temporary accommodation 17·5 per cent of the mothers were under 21 . . . and one-fifth of the children under two (Glastonbury, 1971, p. 49)

We do not know the answers to a number of important questions lying behind this situation. First, why is the age of marriage declining overall? Earlier physical maturation is a factor, but this is set, cruelly, against ever longer schooling and the deferment of an individual's financial self-sufficiency. It is very difficult for any boy to achieve sufficient earning power to support a wife and child until he reaches about 20, whether he is in further education or serving an apprenticeship to a skilled trade. Jobs with good earning prospects which involve neither of these preliminaries are probably fewer and fewer in number, as some kind of formal training is expected of more and more jobs.

Another question is why should working-class life be so stressful? We know that it is in other aspects, for example, satisfaction within marriage (Scanzoni, 1970) and epidemiological studies of mental illness (e.g. Dohrenwend and Dohrenwend, 1969; Brown *et al.*, 1975); but as Hope (1976) has pointed out, we do not know whether this stress is due to lack of material resources, or to the perception that others do not have this lack.

A third question which we should raise is the relative importance in what I have termed in my title "the vortex of disadvantage" of the intertwined factors of early marriage, low social class and relatively rapid family building. Such disentangling of variables calls for a larger-scale investigation than I have been able to describe here. One major American study quoted earlier (Freedman and Coombs, 1966), emphasized the enduring financial disabilities which resulted from starting a family early in marriage.

The fourth question is the most crucial of all: what is to be done? The divorce rate goes up and up, and is marriage to be propped up as an institution, or is it to be made more ephemeral? More counsellors, or easier divorce? Or perhaps harder marriage? It is very easy to marry, easier usually than getting a job and it still only costs a few pounds; I imagine this has been for many people the bargain of a lifetime.

How do we help the weaker sections of the working class? By easier welfare benefits? By encouraging them to help themselves? It is not easy to specify how this could be done. By encouraging them to become more like the middle class? This would be resented by many (of both classes); and would be very difficult to do as it carries strains of its own. Our local authority housing policy, where allocation is based on need, certainly goes in quite the opposite direction. Dependency and need, not self-sufficiency and initiative, are encouraged. Subsequent terms of tenancies often put the tenant into an iron grip and stifle initiative. Selling council houses might go part of the way towards remedying that problem, but one is still left with a waiting list, and houses likely to be sold more often are on "better" estates. The problem of the other estates remains.

How do we help the youthful marriers? Perhaps it is youthful parents who need help most. As Alice Rossi (1968) has pointed out, having a baby has no transitional stage, and it's *your* responsibility. You may have had no training for it. Given the small size of contemporary sibships, today's 20-year-old may never have lived in a home with a baby since his or her own babyhood. Not only is it like advancing from a novice apprentice just signed on at the factory to works manager in one day, but it is a 24-hour-job with no guaranteed tea-breaks and no paid annual holidays, and it is difficult to hand in your notice until the first fifteen years are up.

There is some independent evidence that young brides are aware of the dangers of their situation. One-third of the large sample of teenage brides interviewed by Myra Woolf (1971), (see also Gavron, 1966 for her study of attitudes to family size) thought they had married too young.

Perhaps art has always over-romanticized young love—it is easy to blame the media. After all, the most famous of all romantic heroines, Shakespeare's Juliet, married at 14. But then, look what happened to her . . .

Acknowledgements

The fieldwork described in this paper was undertaken as part of a study of the housing situation of newly-married couples conducted for the Social Science Research Council (Project reference HR2553), whose financial support is gratefully acknowledged.

References

Askham, J. (1975). Fertility and Deprivation: *A Study of Differential Fertility amongst Working-Class Families in Aberdeen*. Cambridge: Cambridge University Press.

Baird, D. and Illsley, R. (1953). Environment and childbearing. *Proceedings of the Royal Society of Medicine*, **46**, 53–59.

Brown, G. W., Bhrolchain, M. N. and Harris, T. (1975). Social class and psychiatric disturbance among women in an urban population. *Sociology*, **9**, 225–254.

Bumpass, L. L. and Sweet, J. A. (1972). Differentials in marital instability (1970). *American Sociological Review*, **37**, 754–766.

Burchinal, L. G. (1965). Trends and prospects for young marriages in the United States. *Journal of Marriage and the Family*, **27**, 243–254.

Chamberlain, A. (1976). Planning versus fatalism. *Journal of Biosocial Science*, **8**, 1–16.

Dohrenwend, B. P. and Dohrenwend, B. S. (1969). *Social Status and Psychological Disorder*. New York: Wiley and Sons.

Dominian, J. (1968). *Marital Breakdown*. Harmondsworth, Middx.: Penguin Books.

Freedman, R. and Coombs, L. (1966). Child spacing and family economic pattern. *American Sociological Review*, **31**, 631–648.

Gavron, H. (1966). *The Captive Wife*. London: Routledge and Kegan Paul.

Gibson, C. (1974). The association between divorce and social class in England and Wales. *British Journal of Sociology*, **25**, 79–93.

Gibson, C. (1975). Divorce and social class. *Marriage Guidance*, **15**, 379–385.

Gill, D. G., Illsley, R. and Hoplik, L. H. (1970). Pregnancy in teenage girls. *Social Science and Medicine*, **3**, 549–574.

Glastonbury, B. (1971). *Homeless Near a Thousand Homes*. London: Allen and Unwin.

Glick, P. C. (1957). *American Families*. New York: Wiley and Sons.

Greve, J., Page, D. and Greve, S. (1971). *Homelessness in London*. London: Chatto and Windus.

Hope, K. (1976). Comments on a study of depression in women. *Sociology*, **10**, 321–323.

Ineichen, B. (1975a). *A Place of Our Own*. London: Housing Research Foundation.

Ineichen, B. (1975b). Teenage wives. *New Society*, 7 August.

Inselberg, R. M. (1962). Marital problems and satisfaction in high-school marriages. *Marriage and Family Living*, **24**, 74–77.

Land, H. (1969). *Large Families in London*. London: Bell and Sons.

Leete, R. (1976). Marriage and divorce. *Population Trends*, **3**, 3–8.

Lowrie, S. H. (1965). Early marriage: premarital pregnancy and associated factors. *Journal of Marriage and the Family*, **27**, 48–56.

Monahan, T. P. (1953). Does age at marriage matter in divorce? *Social Forces*, **32**, 81–87.

Moss, J. J. (1965). Teenage marriage: cross-national trends and sociological factors in the decision of when to marry. *Journal of Marriage and the Family*, **27**, 230–242.

Moss, J. J. and Gingles, R. (1959). The relationship of personality to the incident of early marriage. *Marriage and Family Living*, **21**, 373–377.

Newson, J. and Newson, E. (1963). *Patterns of Infant Care*. London: Allen and Unwin.

Oliver, J. E. and others (1974). *Severely Ill-Treated Young Children in North-east Wiltshire*. Oxford: Oxford Regional Health Authority.

Peel, J. (1972). The Hull family survey, II. Family planning in the first five years of marriage. *Journal of Biosocial Science*, **4**, 333–346.

Peel, J. and Carr, G. (1975). *Contraception and Family Design: A Study of Birth Planning in Contemporary Society*. Edinburgh: Churchill Livingstone.

Pierce, R. M. (1963). Marriage in the fifties. *Sociological Review*, **II**, 215–240.

Rainwater, L. (1960). *And the Poor Get Children*. Chicago: Quadrangle Books.

Rainwater, L. (1971). *Behind Ghetto Walls*. London: Allen Lane.

Rochefort, C. (1961). Marriage. In *Patterns of Sex and Love*. London: Gibbs and Phillips.

Rossi, A. S. (1968). Transition to parenthood. *Journal of Marriage and the Family*, **30**, 26–39.

Rowntree, G. (1962). New facts on teenage marriage. *New Society*, 4 October. Reprinted in *Youth in New Society*. Edited by T. Raison. London: Hart Davis (1966).

Rowntree, G. (1964). Some aspects of marriage breakdown in Britain during the last thirty years. *Population Studies*, **18**, 147–163.

Ryle, A. (1967). *Neurosis in the Ordinary Family*. London: Tavistock.

Scanzoni, J. H. (1970). *Opportunity and the Family*. Glencoe, Illinois: Free Press.

Schofield, M. (1973). *Sexual Behaviour of Young Adults*. London: Allen Lane.

Slater, E. and Woodside, M. (1951). *Patterns of Marriage*. London: Cassell.

Smith, S. M. (1975). *The Battered Child Syndrome*. London: Butterworth.

Woolf, M. (1971). *Family Intentions*. London: HMSO.

Genetic Counselling - Its Genetic and Social Implications

ALAN E. H. EMERY

University Department of Human Genetics,
Western General Hospital,
Edinburgh, Scotland

Introduction

Over the last few decades there has been a gradual decline in the importance of infections and nutritional deficiencies. Their place is being taken by genetic disorders which account for an increasing proportion of morbidity and mortality. At present roughly 1 in 20 children admitted to hospital and 1 in 10 childhood deaths are due to disorders which are largely or even entirely genetic in causation. The prevention of such disorders depends on providing genetic counselling, for parents found to be at risk of having an affected child, and antenatal diagnosis with selective abortion of affected foetuses when this is possible. Here we shall be concerned with some of the possible genetic and social effects of genetic counselling.

Genetic Counselling

Genetic counselling is essentially a process of communication between the geneticist and the individual who seeks advice (Fraser, 1974). It involves a great deal more than merely quoting risk figures. It involves establishing a precise diagnosis, because clinically similar disorders may be inherited differently and have different prognoses, and the mode of inheritance. On this basis the counsellor then discusses with the parents the nature of the disorder, its severity and whether or not there is an effective treatment, and the risks of recurrence. Risks greater than 1 in 10 of having an affected child are by convention considered high and are usually unacceptable to most couples. Finally the various options open to the parents are discussed including contraception, adoption, sterilization, AID and antenatal diagnosis. Of course it has to be remembered that the counsellor is not always a harbinger of woe. In fact many who seek advice prove to be at low risk and can be reassured (Townes, 1970).

The geneticists primary role is to help the parents choose the course of action which seems most appropriate to them taking into account both genetic and social factors. Thus, the counsellor is essentially interpreting medical information in the light of the parents' educational and social background. Though the geneticist does not usually give advice (sometimes called "non-directive counselling") there are situations when he must be prepared to put himself in the position of the parents in helping them arrive at a decision. The more the geneticist understands the background of the parents the more he will be able to help them with difficult problems.

Theoretical effects of Genetic Counselling

There have been a number of theoretical studies of the possible effects of genetic counselling (Mayo, 1970; Smith, 1970; Emery et al., 1971; Motulsky et al., 1971; Fraser, 1972; Holloway and Smith, 1973, 1975; Murphy and Chase, 1975). These effects can be considered when counselling is given either before (so-called *prospective*) or after (so-called *retrospective*) the birth of an affected child. The latter is the more common situation, though additional cases may be prevented by prospective counselling of individuals in the rest of the family. The approximate proportions of cases of genetic disease theoretically preventable by prospective or retrospective counselling are given in Table I (partly

TABLE I

Approximate proportions (per cent) of cases of genetic disease theoretically preventable by genetic counselling

Genetic disorder	Retrospective counselling in sibships	Prospective counselling in the rest of the family	Total	Parental screening
Autosomal dominant	0 (new mutation)	f	f	f
Autosomal recessive	15	5	20	100
X-linked recessive ($f=0$)	10	12	22	66
multifactorial	< 5	2	< 7	100

f = reproductive fitness of affected individuals.

based on Smith, 1970). In the case of autosomal dominant disorders, if the affected child is a new mutant there is virtually no risk to subsequent sibs and the proportion of preventable cases in the family will depend upon the reproductive fitness of the affected individual. In autosomal and X-linked recessive disorders at least 20 per cent of cases could be prevented by genetic counselling.

Clearly genetic counselling will be more effective in unifactorial than multifactorial disorders since the majority of the latter occur sporadically in families. Parental screening would be potentially much more effective in reducing the incidence of genetic disease but apart from a few exceptions (maternal serum alphafetoprotein for CNS malformations, Tay-Sachs disease in Ashkenazi Jews and certain haemoglobinopathies in selected populations) this approach at present is not possible or has not been exploited.

Results on Genetic Counselling

EXTENT OF THE PROBLEM

At present it seems that only a relatively small proportion of individuals at high risk of having a child with a serious genetic disorder are aware of these risks. In a survey of families of individuals referred to this Department for Genetic Counselling, 950 relatives were found to be at high risk yet of these only 138 (15 per cent) had been referred for genetic counselling. Eighty-one affected children were born to parents who a priori were at high risk of having affected children. A proportion of these might well have been prevented by genetic counselling.

From these findings it would seem reasonable to assume that the extent of the problem may be much greater than is reflected by the number of individuals who attend counselling clinics. Even parents attending a medical clinic for a specific hereditary disorder may gain little genetic information unless a particular effort is made on the part of the staff (Taylor and Merrill, 1970).

FACTORS AFFECTING DECISION MAKING

Parents' decision as to whether or not to accept a particular risk is influenced by a great many factors. These include the severity of the abnormality and the availability of effective treatment, educational background and socio-economic factors. Particularly important is the "burden" of the disorder by which is meant the psychological, and to a lesser extent the social and economic problems attendant on having a child with a serious genetic disorder. The concept of burden has been discussed in some detail by Murphy (1973). In some disorders, such as a severe congenital malformation, though the burden is great it is of limited duration and therefore possibly more acceptable than a condition such as Duchenne muscular dystrophy where the affected child lives for many years becoming progressively more incapacitated. There is increasing evidence that parents are perhaps more influenced by the burden of a disorder than the actual risks of recurrence (Carter *et al.*, 1971; Leonard *et al.*, 1972; Emery *et al.*, 1973; Hsia, 1974; Stern and Eldridge, 1975). In any event the interpretation of the risks themselves is very subjective (Pearn, 1973).

Consideration has also to be given to the moral and ethical problems which may arise in the counselling situation (Fletcher, 1972). This is particularly so in the case of a Catholic family faced simultaneously with a number of difficult choices such as family limitation, abortion and sterilization.

Finally besides what might be referred to as "exogenous" factors, there is also the emotional trauma evoked by counselling itself which may interfere with the individuals comprehension of genetic counselling (Sorenson, 1974).

Because of the interaction of these various and complex factors, and because parents are often depressed, anxious and even frankly hostile when they present themselves for counselling (Antley and Hartlage, 1976), it is often impossible to predict an individual's response to counselling. It also makes the evaluation of follow-up studies of individuals given genetic counselling very difficult. Yet these studies are essential if we are to make any attempt to assess the value of the service. Such studies not only allow the counsellor to assess the reliability of the advice given and how far this advice has been followed (WHO, 1969), but also to determine any relatives who are at risk and may also require genetic counselling (Fraser, 1970). It is for this latter reason that Genetic Register Systems have been advocated (WHO, 1972) and initiated (Emery *et al.*, 1974; Emery and Miller, 1976). However, though follow-up studies can be very valuable there is a problem in comparing different centres because of lack of standardization in the methodology of counselling and the different attitudes and personalities of counsellors who may also be very differently qualified. Finally there is the problem of what to evaluate. The comprehension and recollection of risks (education) and the reproductive response to counselling (behaviour) can be assessed relatively easily. But motivations and attitudes to counselling itself are difficult to quantitate and therefore difficult to assess in follow-up studies. Kaback *et al.*, (1974) have attempted to assess the motivations of participants in a voluntary screening programme for Tay-Sachs heterozygotes. Predictably participants who volunteered for screening were younger and on average better educated than those who did not avail themselves of this service. There has so far been no detailed study of the motivations of individuals seen for genetic counselling for hereditary disorders in general.

COMPREHENSION OF COUNSELLING

In assessing the results of genetic counselling it is first necessary to determine if the advice has been understood. A number of studies have been designed to investigate this problem. Some have found that at follow-up the comprehension and/or recollection of genetic information has been poor (Sibinga and Friedman, 1971; Walker et al., 1971; Leonard et al., 1972; Reiss and Menashe, 1972; Lubs, 1973; McCrae et al., 1973). However, it would not be fair to indict genetic counselling on this evidence alone for at least in some of these studies the investigators may have expected too much (Edwards, 1973). Especially if advice is given by a single individual, preferably reinforced on more than one occasion, then comprehension may be much better (Carter et al., 1971; Emery et al., 1972, 1973; Reynolds et al., 1974). Even when illiteracy is high comprehension may be good (Stamatoyannopoulos, 1974) though in general the better the level of education the more likely the genetic risks and their implications will be understood and remembered. One of the most important barriers to a meaningful rapport is the lack of biological knowledge of most couples seen in a clinic (Emery et al., 1973). The importance of genetics in health education has been argued at great length by Childs (1974).

RESPONSE IN RELATION TO RISKS

The response of couples to risks given at genetic counselling has been studied by several investigators (Table II). Several conclusions can be drawn from these studies. It would seem that overall about a quarter of those at high risk are undeterred and roughly the same proportion of those at low risk are unreassured. There is however, considerable variation between different counsellors and even with the same counsellor dealing with different disorders at different times. There is also the problem which is not explicit in all studies, that some couples may have already completed their families at the time of counselling (McCrae et al., 1973).

It seems however, that the greater the burden of the disorder the more likely it is that the counsellor may fail to reassure couples at low risk (Emery et al., 1972). Further, couples may be undeterred by a high risk if the burden is likely to be severe but of short duration (Carter et al., 1971) or if antenatal diagnosis and selective abortion is possible.

The latter has especially been so in more recent follow-up studies (Dennis *et al.*, 1976; Emery, 1976).

TABLE II
Response of couples to risks given at genetic counselling

High risk (> 1/10) undeterred	Low risk (< 1/10) unreassured	Investigator
61/170 (36%)	60/251 (24%)	Carter *et al.* (1971)
[a]4/40 (10%)	[a]5/11 (45%)	Emery *et al.* (1972)
[b]7/46 (15%)	[c]3/15 (20%)	Leonard *et al.* (1972)
10/55 (18%)	17/44 (39%)	Emery *et al.* (1973)
4/19 (21%)	10/40 (25%)	Hsia (1974)
11/27 (41%)	11/39 (28%)	Emery (1976)
[a]7/25 (28%)	[a]4/48 (8%)	Dennis *et al.* (1976)
104/382 (27%)	110/448 (25%)	

[a] Duchenne muscular dystrophy; [b] phenylketonuria and cystic fibrosis; [c] Down syndrome.

MARITAL RELATIONSHIPS

A very disturbing finding in several studies has been the number of couples who were deterred by the high risks of having a child with a serious genetic disorder and in whom contraception failed. Expert contraceptive as well as genetic advice is needed in these cases.

Some have considered that marital disharmony, as assessed by the rate of divorce or separation, is not exceptional among couples seen for counselling (Carter *et al.*, 1971; Reynolds *et al.*, 1974) whereas others have (Emery *et al.*, 1972, 1973; McCrae *et al.*, 1973). It seems that when marital disharmony is evident this is not usually admitted as being a direct result of the disease itself but rather from other factors such as sexual problems consequent on the fear of having an affected child.

Changing patterns in Genetic Counselling

In assessing changing patterns in genetic counselling over any length of time, it is perhaps more valuable to make comparisons between findings at different times with one particular clinic than between different clinics the results of which will be very much influenced by the different ways in which families are ascertained and by the personalities of different counsellors. In Table III are summarized some of the findings from my own clinic covering the periods 1964, 1965–9 and 1970–5. The results indicate that more individuals are now being referred by family doctors, and more often before marriage than in the past. Particularly interesting is the number of self-referrals, individuals who initiated the request for advice themselves, usually the result of having read an article on medical genetics in the press or having seen a television documentary programme. Whereas at one time a sizeable proportion of couples were from the upper socio-economic classes (Carter *et al.*, 1971) who were presumably better informed and therefore more aware of the problems, an increasing number are now seen in the lower socio-economic classes (Table III). These changes in referral, marital status and social class probably indicate an extension of the awareness of genetics within the medical profession and also the general public. However, there has not been any obvious change in the types of disorders seen in the clinic over the last ten years. The increase in the proportion of older mothers can be largely accounted for by women referred for antenatal diagnosis of Down's syndrome because of the increased risk with maternal age. In the past if these risks were unacceptable there was no alternative other than family limitation. With the advent of antenatal diagnosis in the last five years the situation has changed significantly.

TABLE III

Changing patterns in attendance at a genetic counselling clinic
(Results expressed as percentages in each category)

	1964	1965–9	1970–75
Referral			
Consultant	95	63	53
GP	5	27	35
Self	—	10	12
Marital status			
Premarital	0	9	12
Social class			
I/II	—	29	28
III	—	43	48
IV/V	—	28	24
Age			
≥ 40	1	1	7
Mode of inheritance			
UF	45	56	42
CHR	15	8	13
MF	40	36	45

(UF = unifactorial; CHR = chromosomal; MF = multifactorial)

Summary and Conclusions

Theoretical studies indicate that the best scope for preventing genetic disease through counselling lies with the simply inherited (unifactorial) disorders. The follow-up of individuals given genetic counselling confirms this but also indicates that only a proportion of individuals at risk in the population are at present given genetic counselling. It seems that genetic counselling is usually well comprehended by most couples though an important barrier can be a lack of biological knowledge. Most couples act rationally when provided with genetic risks but, because of the large number of complex factors which influence parents in their decision making it is often difficult to evaluate the results of follow-up studies. However, the study of individuals referred for counselling to one clinic over the last thirteen years indicates that more individuals are self-referrals or are being referred by family doctors, more often before marriage, and more often from the lower socio-economic classes. These trends probably reflect an increasing awareness of the value of genetic counselling by the medical profession and by the general population at large, trends which are to be welcomed and encouraged.

References

Antley, R. M. and Hartlage, L. C. (1976). Psychological responses to genetic counseling for Down's syndrome. *Clinical Genetics*, **9**, 257–265.

Carter, C. O., Roberts, J. A. F., Evans, K. A. and Buck, A. R. (1971). Genetic clinic: a follow-up. *Lancet*, **i**, 281–285.

Childs, B. (1974). A place for genetics in health education, and vice versa. *American Journal of Human Genetics*, **26**, 120–135.

Dennis, N. R., Evans, K. A., Clayton, B. and Carter, C. O. (1976). Use of creatine kinase for detecting severe X-linked muscular dystrophy carriers. *British Medical Journal*, **ii**, 577–579.

Edwards, J. H. (1973). Genetic counselling in cystic fibrosis. *Lancet*, **ii**, 919 (letter).

Emery, A. E. H. (1976). Changing patterns in a genetic counselling clinic. In *Genetic Counseling*, pp. 113–120. Edited by H. A. Lubs and F. de la Cruz. New York: Raven Press.

Emery, A. E. H. and Miller, J. R. (1976). *Registers for the Detection and Prevention of Genetic Disease*. New York and London: Symposia Specialists (Stratton Intercontinental).

Emery, A. E. H., Nelson, M. M. and Mayo, O. (1971). Antenatal diagnosis and the muscular dystrophies. In *Actualités de Pathologie Neuro-musculaire*, pp. 13–18. Edited by G. Serratrice. Paris: Expansion Scientifique.

Emery, A. E. H., Watt, M. S. and Clack, E. R. (1972). The effects of genetic counselling in Duchenne muscular dystrophy. *Clinical Genetics*, **3**, 147–150.

Emery, A. E. H., Watt, M. S. and Clack, E. R. (1973). Social effects of genetic counselling. *British Medical Journal*, **i**, 724–726.

Emery, A. E. H., Elliott, D., Moores, M. and Smith, C. (1974). A genetic register system (RAPID). *Journal of Medical Genetics*, **11**, 145–151.

Fletcher, J. (1972). Moral problems in genetic counseling. *Pastoral Psychology*, **23**, 1–14.

Fraser, F. C. (1970). Counseling in genetics: its intent and scope. *Birth Defects: Original Article Series*, **6**,(1), 7–12.

Fraser, F. C. (1974). Genetic counseling. *American Journal of Human Genetics*, **26**, 636–659.

Fraser, G. R. (1972). The short-term reduction in birth incidence of recessive diseases as a result of genetic counseling after the birth of an affected child. *Human Heredity*, **22**, 1—6.

Holloway, S. M. and Smith, C. (1973). Equilibrium frequencies in X-linked recessive disease. *American Journal of Human Genetics*, **25**, 388–396.

Holloway, S. M. and Smith, C. (1975). Effects of various medical and social practices on the frequency of genetic disorders. *American Journal of Human Genetics*, **27**, 614–627.

Hsia, Y. E. (1974). Choosing my children's genes: genetic counseling. In *Genetic Responsibility: On Choosing Our Children's Genes*, pp. 43–59. Edited by M. Lipkin Jr. and P. T. Rowley. New York and London: Plenum Press.

Kaback, M. M., Becker, M. H. and Ruth, M. V. (1974). Sociologic studies in human genetics. I. Compliance factors in a voluntary heterozygote screening program. In *Ethical, Social and Legal Dimensions of Screening for Human Genetic Disease*. Edited by D. Bergsma, pp. 145–163. New York and London: Symposia Specialists (Stratton Intercontinental).

Leonard, C. O., Chase, G.A. and Childs, B. (1972). Genetic counseling: a consumer's view. *New England Journal of Medicine*, **287**, 433–439.

Lubs, M. (1973). Evaluation of genetic counseling in severe X-linked disorders. *American Journal of Human Genetics*, **25**, 48A.

Mayo, O. (1970). On the effects of genetic counseling on gene frequencies. *Human Heredity*, **20**, 361–370.

McCrae, W. M., Cull, A. M., Burton, L. and Dodge, J. (1973). Cystic fibrosis: parents' response to the genetic basis of the disease. *Lancet*, **ii**, 141–143.

Motulsky, A. G., Fraser, G. R., and Felsenstein, J. (1971). Public health and long-term genetic implications of intrauterine diagnosis and selective abortion. *Birth Defects: Original Article Series*, **7**, (5), 22–32.

Murphy, E. A. (1973). Probabilities in genetic counselling. *Birth Defects: Original Article Series*, **9** (4), 19–33.

Murphy, E. A. and Chase, G. A. (1975). *Principles of Genetic Counselling*, pp. 343–372. Chicago: Year Book Medical Publishers.

Pearn, J. H. (1973). Patients' subjective interpretation of risks offered in genetic counselling. *Journal of Medical Genetics*, **10**, 129–134.

Reiss, J. A. and Menashe, V. D. (1972). Genetic counseling and congenital heart disease. *Journal of Pediatrics*, **80**, 655–656.

Reynolds, B. DeV., Puck, M. H. and Robinson, A. (1974). Genetic counseling: an appraisal. *Clinical Genetics*, **5**, 177–187.

Sibinga, M. S. and Friedman, C. J. (1971). Complexities of parental understanding of phenylketonuria. *Paediatrics*, **48**, 216–224.

Smith, C. (1970). Ascertaining those at risk in the prevention and treatment of genetic disease. In *Modern Trends in Human Genetics*—1, pp. 350–369. Edited by A. E. H. Emery. London: Butterworth.

Sorenson, J. R. (1974). Genetic counseling: some psychological considerations. In *Genetic Responsibility: On Choosing Our Children's Genes*. Edited by M. Lipkin Jr. and P. T. Rowley. pp. 61–67. New York and London: Plenum Press.

Stamatoyannopoulos, G. (1974). Problems of screening and counseling in the hemoglobinopathies. In *Birth Defects*. Proceedings of the Fourth International Conference. Edited by A. G. Motulsky, W. Lenz and F. J. G. Ebling. pp. 268–276. Amsterdam: Excerpta Medica.

Stern, R. and Eldridge, R. (1975). Attitudes of patients and their relatives to Huntington's disease. *Journal of Medical Genetics*, **12**, 217–223.

Taylor, K. and Merrill, R. E. (1970). Progress in the delivery of health care. *American Journal of Diseases of Children.* **119,** 209–211.

Townes, P. L. (1970). Preventive genetics and early therapeutic procedures in the control of birth defects. *Birth Defects: Original Article Series,* **6** (1), 42–49.

Walker, J. H., Thomas, M. and Russell, I. T. (1971). Spina bifida—and the parents. *Developmental Medicine and Child Neurology,* **13,** 462–476.

WHO (1969). *Genetic Counselling.* Technical Report Series No. 416, Geneva: WHO.

WHO (1972). *Genetic Disorders: Prevention, Treatment and Rehabilitation.* Technical Report Series No. 497. Geneva: WHO.

Women's Attitudes to Conception and Pregnancy

HILARY GRAHAM

Department of Sociology, University of York
York, England

At first glance, women's attitudes to conception and pregnancy appear to be a well documented area of everyday life. Over the past few years, there has been a series of large-scale surveys which have uncovered a mass of data on the socio-economic correlates of fertility (Bone, 1973; Cartwright, 1970, 1976; Langford, in press; Peel and Carr, 1975; Woolf, 1971; Woolf and Pegden, 1976). In addition to these macro-studies are a number of in-depth investigations elucidating the psychological parameters of the childbearing process (for example Breen, 1975; Chertok, 1969; Goshen-Gottstein, 1966; Klein *et al.*, 1950; Newton, 1955; Scott *et al.* 1956). Together these demographic and psychological studies provide us with detailed information on a seemingly exhaustive catalogue of topics.

On closer examination, however, the apparent profusion of data is somewhat illusory, for the studies, rather than providing complementary analyses of different areas of reproduction, tend to cluster around specific aspects of the childbearing process. In particular, those dimensions which are demographically predictive or psycho-analytically revealing have been singled out as foci of research interest. (The psychoanalytic orientation of much of the in-depth research is apparent in Elaine Grimm's review of the social and psychological literature on childbearing, in Richardson and Guttmacher (1967)). The predictive bias of demographic research and its concern with causal variables is discussed by Cicourel (1964). Although perhaps aiding demographic projection and psychoanalytic theory, this segmenting of women's experiences and the segregating of certain facets for intensive investigation can be seen to have vitiated against the development of a socio-logical understanding of childbearing. For we know a considerable amount about women's family intentions and contraceptive attitudes, about their dreams and anxieties, about their psychosomatic symptoms and their infantile attachments, but we know relatively little about the realities of childbearing as women see and experience them in their daily lives.

The compartmentalizing of experience is encouraged not only by the specificity of the topics under investigation—"family intentions", "sick-role perceptions", "psychological tension"—but by the methods chosen to study them. Researchers rely heavily on traditional quantita-tive techniques—fixed choice questionnaires, personality inventories and projective techniques—to mediate the attitudes and experiences of their informants rather than procedures which allow for more flexibility and negotiation in meanings and categories, for example, participant observation, unstructured interviewing and ethnography. More importantly perhaps, the information derives from the experiences of non-random samples of women. Both demographic and psychological studies have consistently selected certain sub-groups in which to collect their data, test their hypotheses and formulate their theories. The main sub-group for demographic surveys is constituted by married women of childbearing age employed by, among others, Cartwright (1976), Peel and Carr (1975), Woolf, (1971), Woolf and Pegden (1976). The criteria by which respondents for psychologically-oriented studies are chosen tend to be more selective, with samples composed of "normal" married women expecting their first baby emerging as the model group, Breen (1975), Chertok (1969), Colman and Colman (1973), Goshen-et al. Gottstein (1966), Scott (1956). Despite the numerical prepond-erance of these apparently normal samples, other groups within the pregnant population have begun to attract research attention. These are the women whose reproductive behaviour is seen to deviate from socially prescribed norms such as the premaritally pregnant, the un-married mother, the mother with many children and the recipients of abortion. (See Askham, 1975; Land, 1969; Lambert, 1971; Pearson, 1973; Rains, 1971; Roberts, 1966; Royal College of Obstetricians and Gynaecologists, 1972). Unlike the ubiquitous married respondent, these women are selected for study by virtue of their aberrant marital and reproductive circumstances.

The research orientation to selective aspects of childbearing and the methodological preference for homogeneous and non-random samples has had consequences for the kind of interpretative schemas in which the data is set. In particular, these features of the research organization seem to have encouraged perspectives in which the differences and dichotomies among childbearing women are emphasized. For example, marital status, socio-economic position and psychological stability have been adopted as methods by which to differentiate types of individuals and experiences (Davis and Havighurst, 1953; Grimm, 1967; Newton, 1955; Pohlman, 1969; Rainwater, 1960; 1965). The intentionality of pregnancy, whether or not the women meant to become pregnant when she did, has been similarly employed as a means of classifying and theorizing about different groups of expectant mothers (Pearson, 1973; Pohlman, 1969). Again, the focus upon primiparous women (those experiencing childbearing for the first time) has encouraged not only the neglect of the experiences of multiparous women but the generalized notion that pregnancy for these women is both qualitatively different and relatively unproblematic. The assumption that the first pregnancy is intrinsically different from, and more interesting than, subsequent pregnancies is rooted in both psychoanalytic and status passage theories of the transition to motherhood. As Benedek notes

> One would expect the problems to be greater for the woman who is having her first baby, because the change from being a wife to becoming a mother is usually greater than the change from being a mother of one child to be a mother of two (Anthony and Benedek, 1972).

However, as she and other authors have noted

> while the nature of the psychological experience may shift during successive pregnancies, it never alters completely (Colman and Colman, 1973).

This concern with the divisive qualities of childbearing, with such variables as marital status, parity, social class, intentionality, is perhaps surprising given the common physiological context in which reproduction takes place. Looking through the literature, there is little emphasis upon conception and pregnancy as a unifying process in which women of differing social backgrounds and psychic constitutions are drawn together in a shared physiological experience. Rather, the material as a whole creates the impression that childbearing acts as a catalyst upon normally latent or minimal social, emotional and physical differences which are played out on a magnified scale. However, in a study I set up to explore the experiences of 50 expectant mothers (25 primipara, 25 multipara), these differences failed to materialize. Instead, despite the random, heterogeneous nature of the sample, there were significant similarities in attitude to both conception and pregnancy. The study was based on a series of three interviews carried out with each respondent during pregnancy. The sample was randomly selected from mothers booked for a hospital delivery and the class distribution, as derived from husband's/putative father's occupation, reflected the national pattern. Eight of the respondents (6 primipara and 2 multipara) were unmarried at the time of conception.

The results of the study suggested that attention could be usefully refocused on the areas which women, whether primipara or multipara, married or single, planners or non-planners, shared during pregnancy. Therefore, rather than probing deeper into the aspects which reveal dichotomies between individuals and between types of experience, the paper attempts to uncover the dimensions which transcend distinctions of social status. The first section discusses these shared dimensions in the context of women's accounts of conception and the second section looks at the similarities in the way women talked about pregnancy.

Women's Attitudes to Conception

Attitudinal studies of childbearing, whether demographic or psychological in origin, invariably devote considerable space to the question of motivation, and in particular to the analysis of the causes and correlates of intended and unintended pregnancies. In line with this pattern, the women in the sample were similarly asked about the motivational status of their conception (Did you intend to become pregnant when you did?), a question which revealed that 54 per cent of the respondents planned their pregnancy. However, the distinction between the "planners" and the "non-planners" was eroded by other comments elicited in response to this question, and was more forcefully elaborated in replies to less directed questions about the salience of motherhood. (Would you have been upset if you'd been unable to have children? Do you think most women want to have children?) In these replies, themes about the process of becoming pregnant emerged, themes which cross-cut and overshadowed the dichotomy between the "planners" and "non-planners". These themes related to:

1. the personal significance of "having a family";
2. the unproblematic way in which the process of becoming pregnant or "catching on" was perceived;
3. the experience of ambivalent feelings towards the pregnancy and pending maternity.

THE PERSONAL SIGNIFICANCE OF HAVING A FAMILY

Whilst respondents were generally prepared to rate their pregnancy as either planned or unplanned, they frequently went on to discuss and qualify their classification in various ways. For example, one respondent notes that she did not really mean to become pregnant "just then" but continues:

> but well, I always saw myself as having children . . . I always intended settling down and having a family (primipara, "unplanned" pregnancy).

Similarly, another respondent having admitted that her pregnancy was planned, goes on:

> we wanted to start a family as soon as we were married . . . I've always wanted a family (primipara, "planned" pregnancy).

In these comments, the respondents appear to be expanding upon and qualifying their original assessments of the planned or unplanned nature of their conceptions. What is interesting about their qualifications and addenda is that they seem to dissolve the apparently clear-cut distinction between intended and unintended pregnancies. This pattern is not peculiar to women expecting their first baby. Looking at the replies of multiparas, we find again that although they assess the motivational status of their pregnancy differently, they go on to expand and explain their initial characterization in remarkably similar ways:

(Did you intend to become pregnant when you did?)

> It wasn't as though we planned it exactly, but we wanted to have another one and I think its nice for them to be close together in age (multipara, "unplanned" pregnancy).

> "It was planned. I wanted to have a family close together and then they've got each other to play with" (multipara, "planned" pregnancy).

Various explanations can be suggested for the similarity in the planners' and non-planners' accounts of their conception. For example, the qualifications offered by the two non-planners cited above—"I always see myself as having children sometime", "we wanted to have another one", can be taken simply as *post-hoc* rationalizations, as attempts to redefine retrospectively the meaning of their pregnancy in more socially acceptable terms. In such an explanation, the individual's accounts are viewed negatively, taken perhaps as evidence of an indifference to timing and an inability to control their future.

Alternatively, the differing evaluations of pregnancy made by the non-planners could be interpreted in less pathological terms. Their equivocal attitude to their conception as simultaneously "unplanned" and "planned" may reflect not their attempts at rationalization but rather their attempts to cope with the ambiguous meaning of "planning". At first, the respondents appear to employ "planning" in the narrow sense of "family planning"—a mechanistic enterprise aimed at limiting conception to particular, preselected time-periods. Later in their replies, this restricted view of planning seems to be abandoned in favour of one which discusses the personal significance of having children. The apparent inconsistency of their answers hinges around the distinction between "family planning" on the one hand and their "life-plan", in the sense employed by Berger *et al.* (1974), on the other. The planners, too, can be seen to employ this kind of distinction: initially evaluating their pregnancy according to utilitarian criteria such as "We'd been trying for a family", and then expanding on symbolic meaning of childbearing, "I've always wanted a family". While respondents differed in the short-term motivational status of their pregnancy, some were planners and some were non-planners, they invariably agreed on its long-term symbolic significance. With one exception, they all saw having children in positive terms, as a central and taken-for-granted facet of their image of themselves and their future.

Although "having a family" appeared as critical to the present and projected self-identity of 98 per cent of the sample, there were nonetheless differences in the way respondents perceived and accounted for the significance of childbearing in their life-plan. For some women, motherhood was the central role, with marriage providing the institutional framework in which it can most easily be achieved:

> No, it wasn't planned, like, but . . . since I was a kid, before I went to the secondary school, you know, I thought of how I'd grow up and have a little boy called David. That's all I wanted to do. look after this little boy of mine. And, oh yes, I'd have a husband because I knew you needed them to get babies with.

Other respondents reversed this hierarchal ordering of "mother" and "wife", seeing childbearing as a *consequence* of, rather than a reason for, marriage. (These various ideologies of parenthood are discussed by Joan Busfield, 1974). Some in this group saw children in symbolic terms:

> A baby completes a marriage I think. It completes a home, it makes it a family.

or in utilitarian terms, as a source of cohesion and stability for a precarious marriage:

> It brings you closer together . . . to be honest I don't think Mike and I would be together now if it weren't for Sarah.

Whether seen as a cause or consequence of marriage, having children can be seen as central to the women's image of themselves and their future. However, they shared not only a set of perceptions about the centrality and the inevitability of childbearing but also a common attitude towards the process by which conception would occur.

PERCEPTIONS OF THE PROCESS OF IMPREGNATION

Viewed in prospect, as a future possibility, all but a few respondents saw impregnation as an unproblematic, straightforward physiological event. A few respondents with previous menstrual problems doubted their ability to conceive, but for the remainder conception was something which simply happened or could be made to happen to oider. As one respondent put it:

> You decide to go in for a family and you expect it to be, 'boom-boom', and you'll catch on just like that.

Interestingly this typical attitude to *precipitating* conception represents the reciprocal of women's views on *preventing* conception. It was avoiding impregnation that was seen as a hazardous and self-conscious activity, requiring careful forethought and control if it was to be executed successfully. Getting pregnant, by contrast, was rarely treated as something to which a rationalistic attitude was required. For those who found themselves unintentionally pregnant, the process of conception remained at this unproblematic and unarticulated level. However, for those whose pregnancies were intended, it became an event to which one had to adopt a conscious and instrumental orientation. The meaning of becoming pregnant was transformed. Conception was no longer part of the body's unquestioned repertoire of functions: it was something requiring careful time-tabling and the conscientious monitoring of sexual performance. Women no longer talked of simply "catching on" but of "trying for a family", a phrase implying the work-ethic approach which was frequently employed.

Interestingly, however, the adoption of a materialist attitude to conception did not always pay off. Although advocated by family planning organizations as the individually and socially ideal method of family building, for the individuals concerned there were frequently unforeseen difficulties. There were problems of what could be called "method failure", succinctly summarized by one respondent as follows:

> Planning's all very well, but it didn't work for me.

Like over half of the professed "planners", although she articulated her intentions and engaged in the appropriate activities on the appropriate occasions her intended impregnation failed to materialize either at the selected time or in the subsequent three months. Eventually, in a phrase frequently used in such circumstances, she "gave up trying"—gave up, that is, not sexual activity itself but the time-oriented and self-conscious approach she had adopted to it. Her decision to abandon rationalistic family planning and to resort instead to a view of conception as something which "just happens" without human interference rested not only on her failure to become pregnant to order. She, like other "planners", found "trying for a family" created problems for the way other aspects of life were defined. In particular, the mechanics of sex and menstruation became processes to be minutely attended to and reflected upon:

> I'd wait every month, I'd be a bag of nerves a week before, wonder if I'd caught on. And Bob would say, every evening, 'have you started' and he'd be sitting you know, he'd not say anything, but we'd both be thinking the same thing. I kept thinking I'd started and I'd rush to the loo to check, you know. Oh it was terrible! And it'd always come, just when I was beginning to think we'd done it this time . . .

> The doctor told us to try doing it 14 days after me period, you know, and we used to spend all the time in bed, I'm not kidding! Only because it was the right time. I got to the stage where all the time that Dave was there, I didn't let an hour go past, even his dinner hour, I was thinking all the time we should be trying. We used to try all these different positions in case that helped, I often think I'd never have been able to do all that if I'd a baby to look after.

The problems of planning pregnancies, both in successfully achieving impregnation and in adjusting to a new utilitarian approach to sex and menstruation, did not end with conception. Instead, planners faced additional problems in coping with their ambivalent reactions to their new pregnant status.

AMBIVALENCE REGARDING PREGNANCY AND MOTHERHOOD

Paula Hass (1974) has suggested that the dichotomous characterizations of pregnancies as intended or unintended imposes a too-rigid framework around what empirically is a volatile set of attitudes. She argues specifically that classifying a pregnancy as planned or unplanned implies an unanimity between the partners and a stability of attitudes over time that has yet to be empirically verified. She proposes instead that attitudes to childbearing should be reconceptualized to allow for changes in attitude over time and for intra- and inter-personal conflict. The material from the present study provides some empirical evidence for the validity of her model. Respondents not only reported ambiguities and uncertainties about their pregnancy and pending maternity, but their attitudes tended to vacillate between the weeks and months of their pregnancy. For some, it was a differing evaluation of the phases of childbearing that was seen as the source of uncertainty. They liked pregnancy (or early, middle or late pregnancy) but were less enthusiastic about the idea of giving birth or being a mother. As one respondent expecting her second baby, noted:

> I do have mixed feelings about it, even now. Half of me wants it, but the other half, well, I think of all the awful things about babies and I wonder if its a good idea at all.

Such uncertainties were as common among planners as non-planners, with one crucial qualification: non-planners, by virtue of the unintended nature of their pregnancy, had a vocabulary through which to express their ambiguities. As they did not plan to become pregnant, unfavourable attitudes were seen as, if not acceptable, then at least understandable. They could justify, to themselves and to others, their desire to escape from pregnancy, their feelings of hostility for the unborn baby and their forebodings about motherhood.

> I tell him sometimes I don't want it, sometimes I don't you know. I think when its here, perhaps then I will, but I hate seeing myself getting fatter and fatter, you know. I said last night 'I don't want it, I never wanted it.'

Planners, by contrast, although they articulated similar experiences saw themselves caught by the intentionally of their conception. They saw themselves denied, by their own actions, the possibility of verbalizing conflict:

> I often used to think about abortion, even though I planned it. After I was 12 weeks, I went through a bad month or so. I was almost suicidal, I knew it was too late to do anything about it. I never realized really, but its an awful responsibility choosing to have a baby, you know, coming off the Pill to have a baby. I wish it had just happened, you know, I hadn't been on the Pill and it had just happened. It wouldn't depress me as much, I'm sure, if I hadn't planned it.

> Sometimes I really wish I could stop it. You know, when I found out, I was pleased and all, but I started thinking of the alternatives—I even thought of having it adopted . . . I could never tell Steve, oh no, I never would. He'd be really shocked, I mean after all, it was all planned.

This section has focused upon three areas in which the similarities in women's attitudes to conception were more significant, empirically and theoretically, than the differences. In so doing, it has uncovered two problems about the way researchers have typically approached the area. First, the dichotomous classification of pregnancies as planned and unplanned tends to conceal and distort the shared nature of women's intentions and feelings concerning childbearing. Secondly, the positive evaluation placed on planned pregnancies by family planning organizations, as both socially and psychologically preferable to unplanned pregnancies, obscures areas of real difficulty and conflict for those who try to live up to the planned parenthood ideal.

In the following section, the discussion turns from respondents' accounts of the meaning and process of conception to their views upon the dynamics of the pregnancy experience itself. Here, again, it seems that the emphasis upon typologies tends to underplay the existence of a common experimental dimension to pregnancy and, further, to deny certain sections of the pregnant population a vocabulary through which to verbalize their fears.

Women's Attitudes to Pregnancy

As the respondents were all pregnant at the time of first interview, their expectations of pregnancy were already contaminated by actual experiences. Nonetheless, they frequently discussed and contrasted their anticipated image of pregnancy and the reality as they found it. Surprisingly, even mothers with children, found they had "forgotten what it was like" and had re-constructed an image of pregnancy along stereotypical themes. In prospect, pregnancy was regarded as a time in which minor physiological troubles could be expected. However, the minimal discomfort created by these complaints of morning sickness, heartburn, pica, backache and heartburn was to be more than offset by psychological and social compensations. At the psychological level many women expressed the hope that they would experience a sense of fulfilment and well-being; while at the social level they would receive special types of treatment in which their elevated status would be recognized.

In reality, many women reported on the adverse physiological symptoms and the emotional and social advantages which they attributed to pregnancy. In addition, however, they faced physiological and psychological experiences which deviated from this pattern.

Physiologically, many reported symptoms which fell outside the boundaries of their model of pregnancy. These unexpected side-effects fell into two groups. First, there were what might be labelled as the "secret" complaints, the symptoms which were not commonly known about and which women found embarrassing to discuss, such as constipation, piles, varicose veins, vaginal discharge and cystitis. Over 90 per cent of the respondents experienced one or more such complaint. Then, secondly, there were what medically speaking are regarded as "complications" of pregnancy such as high blood pressure, excessive or insufficient weight gain, toxaemia and anaemia. About half the women were diagnosed as having such suspected or confirmed complications at some stage during their pregnancy.

Psychologically, most women found themselves facing feelings and fears which belied their carefree image of pregnancy. It was not simply that their moods exhibited a greater lability than they expected for example, that they were more temperamental, more prone to depression and tearfulness than they expected to be. It was rather that these emotions had an unanticipated focus and direction. They found themselves not only upset or depressed in a free-floating, non-specific way ("for no particular reason") but also prone to worries for which a cause was readily apparent. Frequently these worries related to aspects of the individual's social situation which pregnancy had aggravated or jeopardized, for example, her housing arrangements, her financial position, her marital status, her personal relationships or her employment prospects. In addition, there was a web of issues concerned more specifically with the dynamics of pregnancy. These related to:

1. the nature and management of the women's body;
2. the nature of the child *in utero* and its relationship to the mother's body;
3. the management of time;
4. the nature of childbirth.

These concerns, mentioned over and over again in the course of interviewing, indicated a problematic dimension to being pregnant which was shared by the repondents regardless of the exigencies of their personal situation. In the sample as a whole, all respondents mentioned at least two of these areas and over 70 per cent mentioned all four. These shared problems, for which most women found themselves emotionally unprepared, are discussed briefly below.

THE NATURE AND MANAGEMENT OF ONE'S BODY

Becoming pregnant created for the respondents a series of ambiguities about the nature of their body. They talked about the uncertainties they felt about its beauty or ugliness, about its health or pathology and about its sexuality.

> Physically, to be honest, I think its well, almost grotesque. It seems all out of proportion. I know some think the shape of a pregnant woman is beautiful, her curves and all, but I'm afraid I don't see it.

> I don't let anyone fuss me, its not an illness. I don't expect to be treated like an invalid—in fact I object strongly to it. But things tire me out, its funny, I'm used to taking the dog out, but it really tatters me now. I try and be as normal as I can, but little things tire me out.

These confusions about the nature of pregnancy were intensified by the way in which the women were medically processed during pregnancy. Many commented that whilst within the home it was possible to sustain an image of pregnancy as emotionally gratifying, physically attractive and healthy, but once in the ante-natal clinic such an image was systematically undermined and an alternative model was substituted in which pregnancy appeared as physiological, mundane, unattractive and pathological. (The definition and management of pregnant women in medical settings is discussed by Stoller-Shaw (1974). See also Emerson (1971) and Graham (1976a; b)).

NATURE OF THE CHILD IN UTERO

A second area of concern hinged around the nature and particularly the normality of the unborn child. Over 90 per cent of the sample mentioned their fears concerning deformity and handicap in their baby. It was in the context of this concern with possible abnormality that the uncertainties of the relation between the foetus and its maternal host were highlighted. For many women, the fear of foetal abnormality extended beyond a fatalistic worry that "all was not well" to a concern about deformities which they might have inadvertently created. Thus, it was not simply the possibility of abnormality which was worrying them but the possibility of discovering a personal responsibility for the handicap. As one woman put it, discussing her attention to diet:

> I suppose I felt if he was going to be abnormal and there was nothing I could do about it, that was that. But if it was going to be abnormal through my neglect, then that was inexcusable.

Some women felt their baby was vulnerable to *genetic* malformations because of family history or because the mother considered herself "too old" for successful childbearing. Others felt danger was most prevalent not at the moment of fertilization but during pregnancy when some external, *environmental* teratogen might enter her body and contaminate her child. For some, food, particularly potatoes, was seen as the terotogenic agency. Others saw the consumption of medicines and cigarettes as potentially dangerous, while others were troubled that disease, such as German measles, might be the carrier of abnormality. Another group identified *physical activity* as a risk factor, for example, carrying, lifting and more particularly, sex. For example, one woman discussing sex noted:

> I don't see how it can do the baby any good, do you? I think about it being pressed into my back. I don't like the idea at all.

Finally, were those whose fears related their *reproductive history*, to their recurrent morning sickness which "might be a sign it wasn't right", to previous miscarriages or more particularly to threatened miscarriages which occurred in the course of their present pregnancy. Spontaneous abortion was generally regarded by the respondents, as by embryologists, as "nature's way" of dealing with grossly abnormal embryos. Mothers whose pregnancies were salvaged by medical intervention thus feared that nature had been thwarted. Not only might the symptoms of miscarriage such as pain and vaginal bleeding indicate foetal abnormality but in addition, women worried that the uterine disruption the threatened miscarriage entailed, the loss of blood and the muscular spasms could produce permanent damage in their child.

These concerns about the normality of the unborn child transformed such taken-for-granted activities as eating, drinking, smoking and sex into areas requiring a self-conscious and fastidious approach. In addition, these concerns involved an orientation to time, to the periods of pregnancy when drugs and German measles were most dangerous, when miscarriage and premature labour were most likely. Time became important in another respect in its provision of the developmental milestones such as feeling the baby move, hearing the heartbeat, sensing the descending of the baby's head and so on by which the normal growth and progress of the foetus could be measured.

MANAGEMENT OF TIME

An awareness of the landmarks of foetal development sprang not only from a concern with abnormality but also from a desire to break the long months of pregnancy into psychologically more manageable units. Many women noted the transitional, future-oriented nature of gestation, where one seemed forever to be counting the weeks to the next clinic visit, and marking off the months to "D-day". They noted how time dragged, how they carefully organized the sequencing of such pregnancy tasks as buying and wearing maternity clothes, ordering the pram and preparing the layette so as to achieve a sense of time passing, and yet avoid completing the "passage work" too early. Neither marital nor reproductive status had a consistent influence on the respondent's awareness of time. For example, although first-time mothers appeared to be more sensitive to the physiological and social cues of pregnancy, this was offset by the higher incidence of outside employment which provided an alternative source of interest. Multiparas, although typically less concerned with counting the weeks and noting the landmarks, felt the tedium of being pregnant with other young children to care for.

NATURE OF CHILDBIRTH

Childbirth, the event in which a woman's ambiguities about her body, her fears of foetal abnormality and her concerns with time would be resolved, provided a fourth focus of worry and apprehension. Although women expecting their first baby and particularly unmarried respondents, were generally more fearful of childbirth than mothers with children, these were differences of degree rather than kind. Primipara and multipara, married and single shared a fear of the unpredictable nature of childbirth. They recognized that the duration, the intensity and the outcome of labour and delivery, the possible surgery, injury or even death, were unpredictable variables over which they had only limited control. For primipara, these worries were intensified because of the unknown nature of childbirth: how would they know when they were in labour? what did a contraction feel like? how much pain would they be expected to tolerate? how much could they bear? However, for multipara, knowing the answers to such questions did little to alleviate their concerns about the duration, intensity and outcome of parturition. While primipara feared the unknown in childbirth, multipara feared childbirth precisely because its nature was known and experienced. They talked extensively about their previous confinements and the fears these created for their imminent delivery, fears grounded not only in previous complications (a breech presentation, a caesarian, a post-partum haemorrhage) but in the routine procedures experienced during apparently normal confinements requiring internals, drips, episiotomies and stitches.

It is interesting to note that in the four areas described in relation to individual concerns about her body and her baby, about her approaching confinement and the management of time, the structure and practice of ante-natal care appears to play an important role. Thus, it is not simply that respondents were apprehensive about the physiological processes of pregnancy and childbirth but they were also fearful of the techniques employed to manage and control these processes. They feared not only what their body did during labour and delivery but what was done to their body during that time. Similarly, it is not simply that mothers worried about the beauty and health of their body but they did so in the context of medical definitions which threatened to undermine their self-image. Again, the women did not fear for the normality of their child in abstract for their fear was structured by medical knowledge about embryology and the dynamics of mother–foetus interaction.

Despite the iatrogenic influence in these areas, women rarely felt able to discuss these kinds of fears with medical and paramedical personnel. Nonetheless, the opportunity to discuss some matters of a non-physiological nature was selectively made available to certain categories of respondents. Private consultations with the medical social worker were for example, provided for respondents whose marital statuses appeared as deviant or volatile, for example the premaritally pregnant, the single, the separated and the divorced. However, it was not their avowal of childbirth fears and worries about abnormality that had singled them out for attention. Any opportunity they had to talk about problems intrinsic to pregnancy came only as a result of the purported problematic nature of their extrinsic social circumstances (Macintyre, 1976). Differential treatment was accorded to a second category of respondent, where talk focused more directly on the experience of pregnancy itself. These were the women for whom childbearing was a new and socially-approved experience, the married primipara. (Relaxation classes were open to patients regardless of marital status. However, unmarried respondents felt themselves not "qualified" to join in what they perceived to be a preserve of those who were "doing pregnancy properly". Relaxation sessions were also open to multipara, but again, respondents with children felt inhibited from joining what they considered to be beginners' classes.) Here, consultation was more public and was conducted during ante-natal examination or during relaxation classes. Multipara, although admitting in interview to similar concerns as these "new mothers", found that the clinic medical staff expected emotional problems only from primipara, and this expectation inhibited them from asking what were essentially "beginners" questions. However, although primiparas found the clinic more conducive to the telling of problems, whether in the antenatal check-up or in relaxation classes, the way they and their audience talked tended to distract from the depth and complexity of their concerns. Women would admit to their doctors that they were "a bit worried" about stretch marks or labour pains or German measles and would receive only standardized replies about these specific points (invariably on the theme "Oh you don't need to worry about that"), rather than an invitation to talk about deeper issues. This pattern of specific enquiries and superficial replies was not peculiar to medical encounters but frequently held true when women, whether primipara or multipara, discussed their pregnancy problems with their husband and their families. Only in conversations with close friends with childbearing experience were the "real issues" discussed and about a third of the sample, mainly primipara, professed to having no friends to whom they would turn in this way.

Thus there appears to be a paradox in the notion of a "shared dimension" to pregnancy. Problems surrounding the nature and management of one's body and one's baby, and problems of time and child birth appear to be common to the pregnancy-experience of the women in the sample. However these problems, although shared, are not necessarily communicated either with other pregnant women, with the family or with the doctor, for neither community nor clinic appears to recognize the existence or the salience of such concerns. Even when problem-oriented talk is permitted, women find their worries are side-stepped and trivialized by a ritualized sequence of questions and answers.

It is not only within everyday life that women's attitudes and experiences of pregnancy have been overlooked. Within the academic world, the concern with categories and differences within the pregnant population can be seen similarly to have vitiated against an orientation to the shared experiential qualities of pregnancy, and thus has denied pregnant women an adequate vocabulary through which to verbalize their fears. However, recently, social scientists have become more interested in the biases and limitations of the traditional models of pregnancy and have sought to formulate more meaningful frameworks in which to interpret women's accounts of childbearing (Hass, 1974; Macintyre, 1976; Stoller-Shaw, 1974). I hope this paper has contributed something to this reformulation.

References

Anthony, E. J. and Benedek, T. (1972). *Parenthood: Its Psychology and Psychopathology.* Boston: Little and Brown.

Askham, J. (1975). *Fertility and Deprivation: A Study of Differential Fertility amongst Working-Class Families in Aberdeen.* Cambridge: Cambridge University Press.

Berger, P. L., Berger, B. and Kellner, H. (1974). *The Homeless Mind: Modernization and Consciousness.* Harmondsworth, Middx.: Penguin Books.

Bone, M. (1973). *Family Planning Services in England and Wales.* London: HMSO.

Breen, D. (1975). *The Birth of a First Child.* London: Tavistock Publications.

Busfield, J. (1974). Ideologies and reproduction. In *The Integration of a Child into a Social World.* Edited by M. P. M. Richards. Cambridge: Cambridge University Press.

Cartwright, A. (1970). *Parents and Family Planning Services.* London: Routledge and Kegan Paul.

Cartwright, A. (1976). *How Many Children?* London: Routledge and Kegan Paul.

Chertok, L. (1969). *Motherhood and Personality: Psychosomatic Aspects of Childbirth.* London: Tavistock Publications.

Cicourel, A. V. (1964). *Method and Measurement in Sociology.* Glencoe, Illinois: The Free Press.

Colman, A. and Colman, L. (1973). *Pregnancy: The Psychological Experience.* New York: Herder and Herder.

Davis, A. and Havighurst, R. J. (1953). Social classes and color differences in childbearing. In *Personality in Nature, Society and Culture.* Edited by C. Kluchholm, H. A. Murray and D. M. Schneider. New York: Knopf.

Emerson, J. P. (1971). Behaviour in private places: sustaining definitions of reality in gynaecological examinations. In *Recent Sociology*, No. 2. Edited by H. P. Dreitzel. New York: Collier Macmillan.

Goshen-Gottstein, E. R. (1966). *Marriage and First Pregnancy*. London: Tavistock Publications.

Graham, H. (1976a). The social image of pregnancy: pregnancy as a spirit possession. *Sociological Review*, 32, 291–308.

Graham, H. (1976b). Smoking in pregnancy: the attitudes of expectant mothers. *Social Science and Medicine*, 10, 399–405.

Grimm, E. R. (1967). Psychological and social factors in pregnancy, delivery and outcome. In *Childbearing: Its Social and Psychological Aspects*. Edited by S. A. Richardson and A. F. Guttmacher. Baltimore, Maryland: Williams and Wilkins.

Hass, P. H. (1974). Wanted and unwanted pregnancies: a fertility decision-making model. *The Journal of Social Issues*, 30, 125–167.

Klein, H. R. and others (1950). *Anxiety in Pregnancy and Childbirth*. New York: Paul Hoeber, Inc.

Lambert, J. (1971). Survey of 3,000 unwanted pregnancies. *British Medical Journal*, iv, 156–160.

Land, H. (1969). *Large Families in London*. London: Bell and Sons.

Langford, C. (1977). *Fertility and Contraceptive Practice in Britain: A Report of a Survey Carried out in 1967/8*. (In press).

Macintyre, S. (1976). Who wants babies? The social construction of 'instincts'. In *Sexual Divisions and Society: Process and Change*. Edited by D. L. Barker and S. Allen. London: Tavistock Publications.

Newton, N. (1955). *Maternal Emotions*. New York: Paul Hoebner, Inc.

Pearson, J. F. (1973). Social and psychological aspects of extra-marital first conceptions. *Journal of Biosocial Science*, 5, 453–496.

Peel, J. and Carr, C. (1975). *Contraception and Family Design: A Study of Birth Planning in Contemporary Society*. London: Churchill Livingstone.

Pohlman, E. (1969). *The Psychology of Birth Planning*. Cambridge, Mass.: Schenkman.

Rainwater, L. (1960). *And the Poor Get Children*. Chicago: Quadrangle Books.

Rainwater, L. (1965). *Family Design: Marital Sexuality, Family Size and Contraception*. Chicago: Aldine.

Rains, P. M. (1971). *Becoming an Unwed Mother: A Sociological Account*. Chicago and New York: Aldine/Atherton.

Roberts, R. W. (1966). *The Unwed Mother*. New York and London: Harper and Row.

Royal College of Obstetricians and Gynaecologists, (1972). *Unplanned Pregnancy*. Report of the Working Party. London.

Scott, E. M., Illsley, R. and Thompson, A. M. (1956). A psychological investigation of primigravidae. *Journal of Obstetrics and Gynaecology*, LXIII, 331–343; 494–508.

Stoller-Shaw, N. (1974). *Forced Labor: Maternity Care in the United States*. Oxford: Pergamon Press.

Woolf, M. (1971). *Family Intentions*. London: HMSO.

Woolf, M. and Pegden, S. (1976). *Families Five Years On*. London: HMSO.

Social Factors and Childbirth

ROMA N. CHAMBERLAIN

St Mary's Hospital Medical School, London, England

The death of a mother or her child during childbirth is one of the most devastating tragedies that can happen to a family, but to the epidemiologist it is quite a sensitive measure of the quality of care of mothers and babies.

The fact that adverse social factors are associated with high mortality rates has been known for centuries but the measurement of social factors by the use of social class is, however, comparatively recent. The Registrar General's social class classification was developed to assist in the examination of mortality statistics. It was first used in 1911 and emphasized great variations in death rates between different occupational groups. Comprising 5 groups, social class III is divided into manual and non-manual groups, but in medical statistics this sub-division is often not used.

Mortality during Childbirth and Social Class

Figure 1 has been drawn from figures published in *The Confidential Enquiry into Maternal Deaths for England and Wales*, 1970–1972 (Department of Health and Social Security, 1975). This is a special enquiry conducted by the DHSS into every maternal death that occurs. The mortality rates have been based on 100,000 births and not on the more common 1,000, which are, in themselves, an indication of how safe childbirth has become. In modern society few people have personal knowledge of women who have died in childbirth. To provide sufficient numbers to make statistical comparisons possible, the three years 1970, 1971 and 1972 have been amalgamated, and even then social classes I and II have had to be combined. All mothers who died from maternal causes, including abortion, have been included: the social class of the

married women has been based on their husband's occupation and that
of the unmarried women on their own.

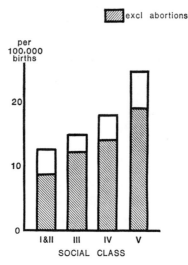

Fig. 1. Maternal mortality per 100,000 births according to social class for England and
Wales, 1970–72.

By definition a baby born dead after the twenty-eighth week of
pregnancy is called a stillbirth or if less than this gestational age, an
abortion. A livebirth is a child who is born alive regardless of gestational
age. However, abortions are not included in the denominator of
maternal death statistics, the rates are based on live and stillbirths. This
can lead to difficulties in the interpretation of maternal death rates from
abortion. For instance, the death rates have not changed much with the
introduction of the Abortion Act because the decline of deaths due to
septic abortion has been, more or less, balanced by the increase due to
therapeutic abortion. However, because the rates are not based on the
number of abortions, the maternal death rates could be the same for a
small number of abortions with a high death rate from one cause, as for
a large number of abortions with a low death rate from another cause.

The pattern of maternal mortality in Fig. 1 shows a steady rise from
social class I and II to IV while that of V seems proportionately rather
greater than might have been expected. Death rates from abortion seem
to be lowest in social class III.

Perinatal mortality is defined as the number of stillbirths and babies
dying within the first week after birth per 1,000 live and stillbirths.
Figure 2 shows the perinatal mortality rate of singleton legitimate

births in England and Wales for the years 1950 and 1973 (Lambert, 1976). The majority of social class statistics relating to births use singleton children only, as classification by the parents' occupations can lead to rather complicated analysis in the case of twins and multiple births.

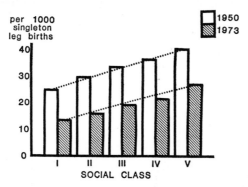

FIG. 2. Perinatal mortality per 1000 legitimate, singleton births according to social class for England and Wales, 1950 and 1973.

The steep social class gradient in mortality appears almost parallel in the two years but in Fig. 3 where the rates have been drawn using a log

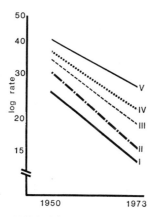

FIG. 3. Perinatal mortality per 1000 legitimate singleton births according to Social class for England and Wales, 1950 and 1973 (log scale).

scale, the decline appears greater among the non-manual than among the manual occupational groups and social class V appears to lag behind more than other classes. However, the Registrar General's classification has been modified between the two years and this might account for the results. Similar differences were found when comparing the Perinatal Mortality Survey, 1958 results with those of the British Births Survey, 1970 (Butler and Bonham, 1963; Chamberlain *et al.*, 1975).

Figure 4 drawn on a log scale shows the rate of decline between the two years for legitimate and illegitimate births (Lambert, 1976). The

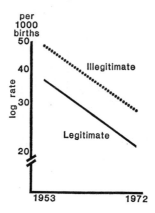

Fig. 4. Perinatal mortality per 1000 legitimate and illegitimate births, England and Wales, 1953 and 1972 (log scale).

perinatal mortality rates for illegitimate births are consistently above those for legitimate births and the rate of decline is the same for both. Similar high rates were found in the British Births Survey, both for mothers who were single and for those who were separated, widowed or divorced, and in both cases the averages were above those for the social class V mothers.

These classic pictures of rising mortality rates with a declining social class grading have been known for many years. Unfortunately the Registrar General does not provide annual statistical information about the effect of social class. Therefore, to prepare this paper the figures have had to be taken from a series of reports, as well as those from the cohort studies, the Perinatal Mortality Survey in 1958 and British Births Survey of 1970.

Many of the factors affecting maternal mortality are the same as those that affect perinatal mortality, but the small number of maternal deaths means that is is not a very sensitive measure, so this paper is mainly about perinatal mortality.

The Measurement of Social Class
Social class is derived from the occupation of men, and it does not provide a good measure for the normal occupations of women. Figure 5

drawn from figures published by the Central Statistical Office (1975) shows the occupation of married women classified by their husband's occupation and by their own. The latter apply to married women who were economically active and retired but excludes the economically inactive such as housewives, while the former are for all married women. The same pattern holds true if the social class of the husband is correlated against the social class of his wife where both are economically active.

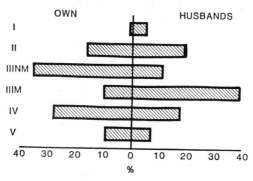

FIG. 5. Social class of married women according to their husbands' occupation and their owm Great Britain, 1971. For definitions see Appendix to the Social Commentary *Social Trends*, No. 6. p. 19 (Central Statistical Office, 1975).

Married women in employment have a heavy concentration in social class III non-manual, while married women by their husband's classification have a heavy concentration in social class III manual. As can be seen very few wives have occupations of their own in social class I compared with their husbands, and more wives than husbands are classified as social class V. Overall 10 per cent of social class I husbands had wives in social class IV or V occupations.

In the same report figures are given for the class of single, widowed and divorced women who are usually classified according to their own occupations. The pattern is similar to that of the married women classified by their own occupation, but there were slightly less in social classes IV and V and slightly more in the non-manual classes of I and II. There were, however, only 1·2 per cent in social class I compared with 0·9 per cent for married women classed according to their own occupations, or 5·3 per cent classed according to their husband's occupations.

Thus, care has to be exercised in interpreting social class data for women in general and particularly for married women. Where data on social class for illegitimate and legitimate births are amalgamated together, as in Fig 1, the distribution into classes will change. The married women will be classified by their husband's occupation with proportionately more births in the manual groups, whereas the single, widowed and divorced mothers will be classified by their own occupations and, therefore, have proportionately more births in the nonmanual groups.

Other Factors Affecting Perinatal Mortality

Table I shows the perinatal mortality rates for singleton legitimate babies in the two national cohort studies, the Perinatal Mortality Survey in 1958 and the British Births Survey in 1970.

TABLE I

Comparison of party distribution and perinatal mortality rates, 1958 and 1970—singleton legitimate only[a]

| Parity | % Distribution | | Perinatal mortality rates | | |
| | 1958 | 1970 | 1958 | 1970 | |
				Rate	% of 1958
0	36·0	35·5	33·6	21·0	63
1	31·2	33·2	23·5	15·1	64
2, 3	23·8	24·2	33·8	22·6	67
4 and over	8·9	7·1	50·5	31·8	63
Total	100·0[b]	100·0	32·0[b]	20·2	63

[a] Taken from Chamberlain *et al*, (1975).
[b] Parity not known included in the totals.

Parity means the number of children the mother has had prior to the present pregnancy. So that "O" parity refers to the mothers who were having their first children. However, the Registrar General was only able to collect information about the number of children in the mother's present or previous marriage. As previous illegitimate children were excluded, the Registrar General's tables included mothers in each parity who may have had more children than their category suggests. Thus, data from the two surveys give slightly different distributions than those of the Office of Population Censuses and Surveys (OPCS).

In this table previous illegitimate children and those from earlier marriages have been included unless the information was not revealed by the mother during the completion of the questionnaire. The mortality rates were higher for those women having their first baby or fifth or later baby, and this pattern was much the same for both enquiries. The proportionate reductions in mortality rates of about one third between 1958 and 1970 were fairly uniform over all parity groups.

Table II shows the perinatal mortality rates in the two surveys according to the age of the mother. In both years there was a higher risk of a perinatal death among mothers under the age of 20 and among those aged 35 and over. The reductions did not vary much but there was some

TABLE II
Comparison of age distribution and perinatal mortality rates, 1958 and 1970—singleton legitimate only[a]

| Age | % Distribution | | Perinatal mortality rates | | |
| | 1958 | 1970 | 1958 | 1970 | |
				Rate	% of 1958
Under 20	5·0	7·7	33·1	25·1	76
20—	28·8	35·4	27·5	16·9	61
25—	32·6	31·9	27·2	18·6	68
30—	20·4	15·7	34·8	20·4	59
35 and over	13·1	8·7	48·7	34·6	71
Not known	0·1	0·6	—[b]	21·3	—
Total	100	100	32	20·2	63

[a] Taken from Chamberlain et al, (1975).
[b] Age not known included in the totals.

differential. Among the less vulnerable 20 to 35 age group the reduction was about two-fifths while for the remainder it was about a quarter.

Table III, from the 1970 British Births Survey, shows that perinatal mortality rates have an inverse relationship with maternal height. The

TABLE III
Maternal height—singletons

Maternal Height	Abortions	Stillbirths	First week deaths	Survivors	Total	Perinatal mortality per 1000 total births
Less than 62 ins.	4	56	44	3,854	3,958	25·3
62–64 ins.	11	88	72	7,142	7,313	21·9
65 ins. or more	8	52	40	5,272	5,372	17·2
Not known	—	3	5	164	172	46·5[a]
Total	23	199	161	16,432	16,815	21·4

[a] This group is likely to be biased by mothers who did not attend for antenatal care and whose heights were not recorded (Chamberlain, et al, 1975).

taller the mother the less likely she is to lose her baby during pregnancy, delivery or the week after birth. Many factors are associated with changes in perinatal mortality but probably the most important is the weight of the baby at birth. Babies weighing 2,500 g or less are at a very much higher risk than those of any other weight.

Small mothers, the extremes of age and the extremes of parity are associated with low birthweight babies, as is smoking during pregnancy and maternal illness. On average, girls weigh less at birth than boys. Not only, however, are all these factors associated with low birthweight and therefore with high mortality rates, but each probably has an independent effect as well as being intercorrelated with the other factors.

Association of Social Class with the Other Variables Influencing Perinatal Mortality

Table IV gives the perinatal mortality rates according to the social class and age of the mother. These figures and those in Table V were supplied by the OPCS. For each of the common age groups there is a consistent social class gradient, but social class III manual rates are below those for class III non-manual rates for mothers under 20 and are above social class IV for mothers aged 40 and over.

TABLE IV

Perinatal mortality rates per 1000 total births by maternal age and social class, 1973 (singleton legitimate births only) : England and Wales

	I	II	III Nm	IIIM	IV	V	Total[a]
Under 20	19·9	17·2	22·4	20·1	26·9	29·7	23·0
20—	14·2	14·1	16·2	17·5	19·2	23·1	17·5
25—	12·2	14·8	16·1	17·9	18·7	23·0	16·6
30—	13·8	16·0	17·1	23·3	25·4	34·5	20·4
35—	23·2	19·5	27·6	30·4	29·9	33·4	27·1
40 and over	31·0	37·4	35·9	47·2	43·3	50·2	42·8
Total[b]	13·9	15·6	17·3	19·7	21·8	26·8	18·9

[a] Includes Armed Forces and others not included in social classes I to V.
[b] Includes those where the age of the mother was not known.—From OPCS figures.

In the same year, 1973, 42 per cent of the mothers of legitimate births were under 25 years of age, including 8·5 per cent under 20: whereas 67 per cent of the mothers of illegitimate births were under 25 years including 36 per cent under the age of 20. Table V shows the perinatal mortality rates for illegitimate births according to the age of the mother.

TABLE V

Perinatal mortality rates per 1000 total births by maternal age, 1973 (singleton, illegitimate births): England and Wales

Age	Rate
Under 20	26·1
20—	22·4
25—	25·0
30—	25·4
35—	40·7
Over 40	54·1
Total[a]	26·3

[a] Includes those where the age of the mother was not known—From OPCS figures.

The rates for those under 20 years (36 per cent of the births) were lower than those for the social class IV married mothers in the same age group, and it was not until the age of 25 years and after that the rates exceeded those of social class V. The odd peak occurring in social class V 30–34 year old mothers of legitimate children did not occur in the illegitimate births. Among the 6 per cent of illegitimate births which occurred at the age of 35 years and later, the death rates increased sharply with age and were above those for social class V legitimate births.

Although there are variations in the rank order from parity 3 onwards, there is a consistent social class gradient within the more common maternal parities for legitimate births (Lambert, 1976). Statistics are not collected about the parity of mothers with illegitimate births but presumably they are heavily weighted with mothers having their first babies. From these figures it is probable that the high overall death rate of illegitimate births can be mainly accounted for by a preponderance of young mothers having their first babies and particularly high death rates among the older mothers.

Figure 6 reproduced from Butler and Alberman, (1969) shows the combined effect of maternal height and socio-economic status on perinatal mortality in 1958. The proportion of tall mothers was greatest among those whose husbands were in the professional groups and smallest amongst the wives of unskilled workers, with a steady declining gradient between. At the same time mortality rates were highest among the short women and lowest among the tall women. This occurred in each socio-economic group. Nevertheless, the perinatal mortality rates among the short wives in the professional group were still higher than those of the tall wives of unskilled workers.

Figure 7 taken from the British Birth Survey shows the effect of social class on the birth weight of the child for each gestational age. These differences become more marked as pregnancy progresses, so that babies from the lower groups born after about the thirty-sixth week of pregnancy tend to be small-for-dates compared with those of the upper groups.

PERINATAL   MORTALITY   SURVEY

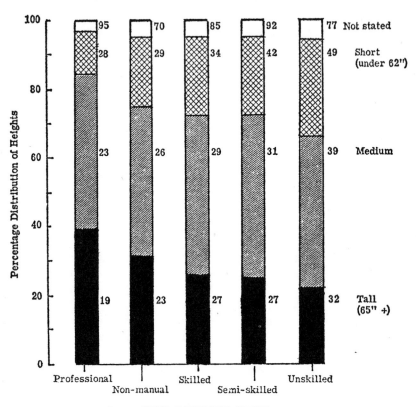

SOCIO-ECONOMIC GROUP

Fig. 6. Distribution of materal heights by socio-economic status of husbands (columns) and perinatal death rates by height and socio-economic group (figures). Perinatal Mortality Survey, 1958.

However, Goldstein, using the Perinatal Mortality Survey data carried out an analysis of variance with several variables and showed that the apparent relationship of high maternal age with high birth-weight, and low social class with low birthweight appeared to be due to their correlation with other factors such as maternal illness, height, parity and smoking habits (Butler and Alberman, 1969). It has been suggested that the form of the birthweight distribution might be inappropriate for application of the standard statistical techniques (Pethybridge *et al.*, 1974). So the problem of whether social class has an independent effect upon the growth of the foetus or whether the association is merely the result of other factors has not been entirely resolved.

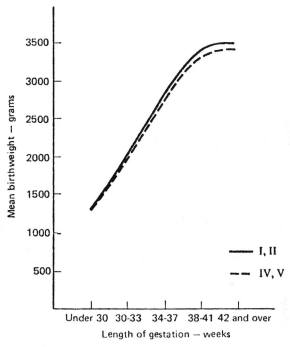

Fig. 7. Mean birthweight for length of gestation according to social class, singleton births. British Births, 1970. (Chamberlain *et al*, 1975).

Effect of Using Cross-sectional Studies

There is an increasing mortality with declining social class and both these factors are associated with low birthweight. Many factors, all inter-related, are associated with high maternal and perinatal mortality rates. Social class appears to measure the interaction between many of these factors, so that groups of mothers with different childbearing patterns appear to dominate in each social class and bring their mortality experience with them. At each age death rates are higher among the manual groups and a similar pattern for death rates is found for each parity group.

All these findings are based on cross-sectional studies, whether from official or other statistics. Non-manual groups have a later pattern of marriage and, therefore, the mothers in these groups tend to be older than those in the manual groups. The 1 in 30 national sample of all births from 1970–1972 showed that in the non-manual groups 60 per cent of the births occurred to mothers aged over 25 compared with about 50 per cent to mothers in the manual groups (Central Statistical Office, 1975). If average family building starts at different ages in different social classes and the ultimate family size and possibly the rate at which the family is built up also varies with social class, then data derived from cross-sectional studies cannot take this into account, and analysis of large scale longitudinal or cohort studies might well give different answers.

In the 1970–1972 national sample a difference of $4\frac{1}{2}$ years was found between the ages at which the married women in social classes I and V had their first live birth within marriage. On average, those in social class I were 26·3 years and in social class V, 21·9 years (Central Statistical Office, 1975). Thus in social class I the first baby, who is usually considered to be at a high risk, is postponed until after the age of 20 when the mother is at a more favourable age for childbearing.

Whereas in social class V not only is the first baby more likely to be born when the mother is at a more vulnerable age, but the younger she is the more likely she is to have further children and eventually a larger family. If, therefore, the longitudinal data is in agreement with the cross-sectional data, these mothers are more likely to have a perinatal death.

Previous pregnancy experience probably causes considerable self-selection in the decision whether to have another child, and James has pointed out the difficulty of interpreting data concerning the association of foetal wastage with birth order, maternal age and birth interval drawn from cross-sectional studies, as the fertility of the mother cannot be taken into account. For instance, after working on a cohort study he suggested that there was no causal connection between short birth intervals and stillbirths, merely that women most prone to bear still-births tended, on average, to be more fertile than other women and, therefore, had shorter birth intervals (James, 1976).

Again cross-sectional studies do not take social mobility into account and social class based on occupation tends to change as the husbands get older. In the 1971 census, between the ages of 15 to 24 years, 3·4 per cent of men were in social class I but for ages between 25 to 34 this rate was doubled to 7·1 per cent; 9·6 per cent were in social class II in the first decade and this rose to 17·1 per cent in the next ten years. At the other end of the scale 8·6 per cent were in social class V between the ages of 15 to 24 and between the ages of 25 to 34 this fell to 6·1 per cent. On the other hand, the proportion in social class IV remained relatively unchanged, being 15·8 and 14·8 per cent respectively for the younger and older groups (Central Statistical Office, 1975). Some of the reasons for these changes are that younger men in professional non-manual grades are under-represented, as they may be in training and, therefore, economically inactive or may be working in lower manual grades while in training but later are promoted to higher positions, either in manual or non-manual grades.

Many of the mortality differences between social classes are probably accounted for by differences in the population structure and; therefore, lie more in their child-bearing and family formation patterns than in their medical care or living conditions; although, it could be possible that mortality differences in the biological characteristics of age and parity are reflecting social class differences.

Other Factors Associated with Social Class

Lower social groups are usually associated with poor housing, overcrowding and poor nutrition, and these lead to an increase in the likelihood of illness and infection. In the past this was the classic background of infant mortality and morbidity and it probably still holds good for the older babies. However, the fact is that the majority of babies who are dying from perinatal causes die within a few hours or days of birth and, with a few exceptions, are born in hospital and never see the houses or the living conditions of their parents. For over 90 per cent of births in this country now takes place in institutions, usually National Health Service hospitals or general practitioner units but also in other hospitals and maternity homes. Few of these babies die from any form of infection. The admission for hospital care is no longer governed by economic considerations, and unlike the reports of the 1940s, the cost of inpatient care to the mother is no longer a factor.

However there are still, at least, two other important social factors. One is the failure to use the services and the other is, possibly, poor nutrition.

In the Confidential Enquiry into Maternal Deaths, the failure to use the care provided was considered to account for an appreciable proportion of the deaths where the tragedy might possibly have been avoided. Some pregnancies were concealed, either because the mother was single or because they were the result of extra-marital relations. Pre-eclamptic toxaemia of pregnancy is a condition which can be detected by carrying out regular pre-natal care. But the signs by which the physician or midwife detect it usually occur pre-symptomatically, so that the patient may feel fit and well and be unaware of the risk. Consequently the mother may feel that her home and family are more important than the need for her to enter hospital. Such women may come from any social group, but it is likely that help may not be so easily available or acceptable among those in poorer economic circumstances, especially if the mother already has a large family to care for. Alternatively, fear and ignorance may make it difficult for her to appreciate the need to attend for regular pre-natal care, and some will fail to do so despite messages and letters. Again differences in attitude to medical care and difficulties in communication are more likely to be problems among the lower social groups. The number of maternal deaths caused by these factors is very small but the outcome may be not a maternal but a foetal or perinatal death.

Secondly, the majority of enquiries into perinatal death over many years have suggested that poor maternal nutrition may be a factor in the causation of perinatal deaths. Persistently this has been suggested. But it is difficult to quantify the extent to which poor nutrition could be a contributory factor. For mothers born in this country, the malformed pelvis caused by rickets was in the past a reason for many difficult and long labours. Nevertheless, mothers in the lower groups are shorter and this is unlikely to be entirely due to genetic reasons. It may be possible that in some, under-nutrition in early childhood has resulted in permanent stunting and, in order to match the size of the baby to the pelvis, nature tends to retard the growth of the child, so that at birth the babies are smaller and, therefore, more vulnerable.

In the British Births Survey we found that the perinatal mortality rate was half as high again for families where the father was unemployed compared with those where the father was employed. The proportion of unemployed fathers in social class V was five times higher than those in social class I (British Births Survey. Unpublished data). These figures referred to 1970, the number of unemployed men was small and the differences were not statistically significant. Nevertheless, they may indicate another social group who might be vulnerable.

Thus, having started with a simple picture of social class differences in mortality analogous to a theory of gravitation by which the lower she sinks in the social class scale the greater the hazard to the mother and the baby, I have now amended it to a theory of relativity.

Acknowledgements
The material from Government publications is reproduced with the permission of the Controller of Her Majesty's Stationery Office.

The data and diagram from the British Births Survey are reproduced by permission of the National Birthday Trust Fund and William Heinemann Medical Books Ltd.

The diagram from Perinatal Problems is reproduced by permission of Churchill Livingstone Ltd.

References

Butler, N. R. and Alberman, E. D. (1969). *Perinatal Problems*. Second Report of the British Perinatal Mortality Survey. Edinburgh: Churchill Livingstone.

Butler, N. R. and Bonham, D. G. (1963). *Perinatal Mortality*. First Report of the British Perinatal Mortality Survey. Edinburgh: Churchill Livingstone.

Central Statistical Office (1975). *Social Trends*, No. 6. London: HMSO.

Chamberlain, R., Chamberlain, G., Howlett, B. and Claireaux, A. (1975). *British Births 1970*. Vol. 1. *The First Week of Life*. London: William Heinemann Medical Books.

Department of Health and Social Security (1975). *Report on the Confidential Enquiry into Maternal Deaths in England and Wales, 1970–1972*. Health and Social Subjects 11. London: HMSO.

James, W. H. (1976). Birth order, maternal age and birth interval in epidemiology. *International Journal of Epidemiology*, **5**, 131.

Lambert, P. (1976). Perinatal mortality: social and environmental factors. *Population Trends*, **4**, 4–8.

Pethybridge, R. J., Ashford, J. R. and Fryer, J. G. (1974). Some features of the distribution of birthweight of human infants. *British Journal of Social and Preventive Medicine*, **28**, 10–18.

Changing Social Attitudes to Childhood

MARGARET E. WOOD

The City University, London, England

In approaching a study of the changing social attitudes to children, may I ask you at the outset to bear a number of factors in mind. First, all that will be said by me today applies to the culture of so-called western society, and even within this society there have been, and still are, at least marginally different attitudes to children in different countries. Then, nearly everything that has been written and pictorially illustrated about childhood, about child-rearing, and about the family has been written by, written for, and written about people belonging to the middle and upper social classes. Even the baby books published in the 1920s and 1930s assumed that their readers were at least middle class. We have knowledge of the conditions under which working-class children have lived, but this knowledge is meagre when compared to our knowledge of the attitude of upper-class adults towards children. It is only relatively recently that specific differences have been noted between customs of child rearing, which vary not only according to social-class membership in one country, but also according to different geographical areas within that same country (Newson and Newson, 1963). Another point to remember is that most of what has been written about childhood and about attitudes to children before the nineteenth century appears to have taken it for granted that by "child" one, in fact, means "boy"! It is common knowledge that certain privileged girls, such as Elizabeth I and the daughters of Sir Thomas More, received an education equal to that of their brothers, but it was not until the eighteenth and nineteenth centuries that girls went to school, though a few girls' schools did exist earlier; but generally we do not know very much about society's attitude in the past specifically to girls, though we do know that the birth of a girl was nearly always unwelcome. Finally, although it is possible to trace a pattern of a more-or-less consistent change of attitudes towards children from medieval times to the present day, there are, nevertheless, not infrequently different viewpoints discernible within any one historical period, and there have also been some remarkable "swings of the pendulum" from one period to another.

According to de Mause (1974) this pattern of consistent change can be seen in six major "modes", as he calls them, which, he considers,

> represent a continuous sequence of closer approaches between parent and child as generation after generation of parents slowly overcame their anxieties and began to develop the capacity to identify and satisfy the needs of their children (p. 51).

I must stress that de Mause's views regarding the particular emphasis which each historical period carries in relation to parental attitudes to children is a highly personal one. These modes were, first, the mode of "infanticide", which prevailed until approximately the fourth century, though the practice of exposing children, nearly always girls, and leaving them to die, seems to have been carried out well into the nineteenth century. The mode of infanticide was, according to de Mause, followed by the mode of "abandonment", practised until the thirteenth century. Children were handed over to others to be brought up. The third mode, which lasted until the eighteenth century, he has termed the mode of "ambivalence". Children now began to enter into their parents' emotional life. This mode was succeeded by the "intrusive" mode, which was characterized by the parents' attempt to conquer their child's mind and will. In the nineteenth century and the first half of the twentieth century the need to raise a socially-acceptable human being seemed to parents of first importance, and de Mause has termed this mode of upbringing the "socialization" mode. The final mode, the "helping" mode, which de Mause says is now current, signifies an awareness of the child's actual needs, and an attempt by parents to meet these needs. However, the manner in which the parental activities and attitudes associated with this mode is described by de Mause implies that "helping" is seen as being almost synonymous with what has been termed "permissive rearing"; but whereas most child psychologists will agree that it is wholly admirable to be aware of children's needs and to attempt to meet these at various stages of development, this does not necessarily mean applying permissive rearing methods. We shall return to this theme later. So we have a pattern of attitudes which ranges from the unsentimental disposal of unwanted children to the devotion of much time, energy and loving thought to their upbringing.

It is difficult to separate the changing concept of childhood from the evolution of the family. The historically-modern family is a unique institution. Medieval families of all classes sent their children at quite an early age to other families for service, for training, or for education; children from seven or eight years of age thus shared in both the domestic and the professional life of adults, but of adults who were not their parents. Since children left their home early in life they did not have much contact with their own parents or with their siblings, and so the pattern of relationships between family members was clearly different from that of the often somewhat introverted and emotionally-close families of later times. This early removal from home strongly reminds one of the still current fashion among certain classes of sending boys away to preparatory school at a very tender age.

However, during the later middle-ages parents generally preferred to keep their children nearer to them, to remove them from the exclusive influence of other adults, and to allow them to obtain their education while living at home. Thus it is clear that as schooling became a more usual experience for many children, the family, as a child-centred institution, came into being.

It is surprising to realize that in most paintings of medieval art children are shown as if they were miniature adults, though it seems that artists were able to depict children realistically and not infrequently did so, even in early-medieval paintings (Lasareff, 1938); but one feels that those paintings which showed children as small adults, with the same head–body ratio as adults, more accurately reflected the prevailing feeling that after seven years of age, or so, children were merely smaller and less experienced adults, but in no important way different from grown-up people. During the seventeenth century three concepts of childhood seemed to have been held more or less simultaneously: that children were unimportant and should be ignored; that they were playthings, to be petted and fondled for the pleasure they gave; and that childhood was a time of ignorance, irrationality and levity, and that adults had to learn to understand this period of life in order to correct children's behaviour (Ariès, 1962). Attitudes about how this "correction" should be carried out varied. Lord David Cecil reports that during the reign of Elizabeth I in the sixteenth century Lord Burghley, who "kept a school for young noblemen", believed that pupils were more easily led by kindness than by severity; he also took a great interest in his own children, they "occupied much of his attention", and he took pains about their education (Cecil, 1973). Others, however, believed in a sterner discipline. It is interesting to note that the difference in viewpoint between those persons who advocate a "hard" method of bringing up children, and those who advocate a "soft" method, is not something which only exists in the twentieth century!

There have, of course, always been enlightened people, such as John Locke and Rousseau, who viewed the period of childhood in an understanding way. John Locke especially was remarkably modern in his view of children, and his book *Some Thoughts Concerning Education*, published in 1693, was well-known in other countries of Europe too. He was perceptive enough to realize that for the young child work and play were synonymous, and that much could be taught through play; but it seems certain that his appreciation of the important differences between children's minds and adult minds was exceptional. Locke also disagreed with flogging and beating (Plumb, 1975). But beatings were the generally accepted rule from the earliest times as an aid to child rearing, and de Mause mentions that the earliest record he could find of children who were not beaten at all dates from 1690.

Speaking generally, the period before the eighteenth century at least was grim for most children; indeed, only a relatively small proportion of those born survived to endure life for long. The child mortality rate prior to the civil registration of births is variously estimated for the seventeenth century as being 25 per cent before one year of age, with 50 per cent of all children dying before they reached teenage, to, as late as the mid-eighteenth century, 75 per cent of all children dying before they reached five years of age (Newsom, 1967). In a recent biography of Mrs Gaskell (Gerin, 1976), who was born in 1810, mention is made of the fact that she was the youngest of eight children, six of whom had died before she was born! Although such a death rate in one family was probably not common, it may well not have been very abnormal. Elizabeth Newson (1967), considers that the early death of children inevitably influenced attitudes to child rearing, and that only when infant mortality had been very considerably reduced in the mid-nineteenth century did a major attitude change towards children occur. Plumb (1975) however, suggests that a fundamental change occurred in parental interest in children in the eighteenth century. His findings are that people then generally began to feel differently about their children, and that this change of attitude was due not only to children living longer than previously, but because they were more healthy and their parents also were better off. He has described how, while prior to the 1740s there were very few books available specially produced for children apart from grammars, by the end of the century a mass of titles, spanning a wide range of subjects, appeared each year. He writes that by 1780

> there was no subject, scientific or literary, that had not its specialized literature designed for children . . . (p. 83).

It is interesting to note that the less affluent working-class parents also bought these books. The number of provincial theatres which were built at this time in England also meant that children could be, and, indeed, were, taken to the theatre and to concerts; drawing masters were engaged, and a number of educational entertainments could be enjoyed (Plumb, 1975). Because of the many books which were now available, the family outings and entertainments which were possible, and the variety of educational pursuits which could be followed, it is clear, as Plumb writes, that life for the middle-class child of the 1780s was very different from that lived by the child a century earlier. No doubt the founding of the Royal Society in 1660, and the excitement engendered by the various scientific discoveries made during the following decades, contributed in the ensuing century both to an interest in education and an appreciation of its advantages.

The period of childhood was also by now much more clearly specified, so that a person was no longer merely an infant or a child before becoming adult. During the medieval period people had been much concerned with the importance of age and its relation to man's changing position throughout life, but as far as the early period of life was concerned even Shakespeare's *Seven Ages of Man* allowed only for "infancy", the "whining schoolboy", and then "the lover". The meaning of the word "child" related then as much to the dependence of a person on others as to his chronological age. However, Ariès (1962) tells how Pascal's pupils in the eighteenth century were described as being either "little ones", "middle ones", or "big ones", and it is noteworthy that as we move from the eighteenth century to the nineteenth century childhood begins to be seen as an experience which is different not only between infancy on the one hand and adulthood on the other, but different also between one period within childhood to another. Yet just at this time children were once more sent away to school, and their child life separated from their adult life. This period saw the development of the boarding school; and despite a greater interest in children and in their education, much more physical punishment was meted out than in previous decades, particularly in schools.

This separation of all the childhood years from those of the rest of a person's life still shows its effect today in society's attitude to adolescence. Margaret Mead (1928) suggested that in some primitive societies, at least as she observed them in pre-war days, children were given tasks of increasing complexity and responsibility suited to their increasing age, and adulthood was achieved gradually as childhood was equally gradually relinquished. The state of "adolescence", she suggested, did not exist as it exists in western societies. In our society, adolescents seem to live in a kind of temporal no-man's land, where adults, according to their whim or the situation, alternatively accuse young people of being irresponsible for their age, or tell them they are too young to do something they may wish to do; and while they are physically mature, they are economically still dependent.

By the mid-nineteenth century infant mortality was down to 15·4 per cent. By now a large body of literature on child-rearing problems had appeared in the USA. Sunley, in Mead and Wolfenstein (1955) has outlined the reasons which led to the particular kind of child-rearing advice which was given to parents during this period. Already by the end of the eighteenth century parents had a clear idea of the kind of adult they sought to raise, but in the nineteenth century parents appear to have had a greater confidence in being able to achieve their aim. It is interesting to note not only how the values of society, then as now, are inevitably reflected in what parents and educators seek to achieve when bringing up children, but also how at this particular time—the mid-nineteenth century—the optimism which sprang from a strong feeling that man could control his environment and influence his future also gave him the belief that he could "shape"—to use a later, "Skinnerian", term—the character of the children in his care. Such confidence, later reinforced by Pavlovian ideas of conditioning, lasted well into the next century.

In the mid-nineteenth century, however, as Sunley further points out, Calvinistic religious ideas were particularly influential in the United States in determining the kind of adult person parents wanted their children to become. Such a person should be

> a moral, honest, religious, independent individual, who could take his proper place in society, (p. 51).

Dwight, quoted in Mead and Wolfenstein (1834) said that

> no child has ever been known, since the earliest period of the world, destitute of an evil disposition—however sweet it appears (p. 159).

Because the likelihood of a child dying in 1850 was still seven times as great as it would be a hundred years later, it was important that the child should be trained from earliest infancy to learn to overcome its "evil disposition", and to earn Grace, and avoid eternal damnation.

The child's will had thus to become pliant to parental and religious demands. Both Plumb (1975), writing about the development of schools in the eighteenth century, and Sunley (1955), concerned with the new child-rearing advice given to American parents in the nineteenth century, make the point that a scholastically-successful child and a well-mannered child, enhanced parental standing in society. A modern parallel consists in the great importance which until only recently, was placed by many parents on their children passing the "eleven plus" examination, often as much for considerations of family prestige as for academic reasons.

Judith Temple (writing in Temple, 1970) refers to the fact that in Victorian England—

duty was the foundation of all family relationship

and that

childhood seems to have been a condition to grow out of and master (p. 14).

The middle-class child who appeared in Victorian fiction for children

could never escape from the clutches of his parents or his conscience, (Temple, 1970, p. 14).

Green's Nursery Album of 1848, quoted by Nigel Temple, contains poems ostensibly written by children, which are almost unbelievable in the degree of eulogy expressed for both parents, and the admission of follies of various kinds by the children. For the Victorian child, parents must have appeared only slightly lower in the hierarchical structure of their society than God himself. No wonder Freud wrote (1916) that the major task which every individual had to accomplish in life was to free himself from his parents! It has been suggested that friendship between parents and children in such an authoritarian atmosphere in middle-class families was not possible but Thompson, in a study he began in 1969 put forward the view that the distant relationship which was in vogue even later in the nineteenth century between parents and children in the middle-classes did not exist to the same extent in working-class families; and Thompson also remarks on the relative absence of the physical punishment of children in working-class families of the period.

The idea that children could be trained to exhibit the character and personality determined by adults was reinforced by Pavlov's work once it became known in the English-speaking world in about 1912. Watson, who did so much to popularize Pavlovian ideas, is famous for his remark that he could condition a child to become whatever he, Watson, desired it to become; and the ideal end-product of child-training in the early part of the twentieth century was not dissimilar to the mid-nineteenth century ideal. Character training was still the important aim, and Sir Truby King used the ideas inherent in conditioning to evolve a system of child-rearing which was based on the establishing of a regular regime of eating, sleeping and defaecating. If good bodily habits could be established in the child it was assumed that good mental habits could also be formed, and among these "good mental habits" was to be the realization by the young baby that adults were in charge of his life, and that his desires would not be indulged. The notion that a child's "desires" might be dictated by his needs does not seem to have been appreciated. One aspect of children's spontaneous activity which troubled parents at the turn of the century, and later, was their auto-erotic behaviour. This was considered dangerous, and, as is well-known, masturbation in particular was thought to have quite dreadful consequences. Even as recently as the late 1940s I saw a mother sew up the sleeves of her baby's garment so that the child could not touch his own body! It is interesting that, as Plumb (1975) suggests, though little is known historically about attitudes to sex, already in the eighteenth century

> the world of sex was to become a world of terror for children . . . (p. 92).

Although character training was still considered important, the baby books of the 1920s and 1930s, especially those written by psycho-analytically-orientated writers, began to be more concerned with bringing up children who became mentally healthy, although probably mental health was by now more-or-less synonymous with having a "good" character; but whether mental health was best produced by inculcating good habits, as advocated by Truby King, or by being effectively conscious of the child's psychosexual development, was a question of dispute. In 1929, only shortly before the publication of Truby King's manual, Susan Isaacs, a Freudian child specialist, published her *Nursery Years*; the only point of agreement between these two books, however, seems to have been the importance of early childhood experience to later development. The difficulty for middle-class parents from about 1930 onwards was that, able to read about child-rearing practices from both points of view, they received no help in deciding which was more likely to be the true point of view! Families were now smaller, so that parents could give much more attention to their children, and, having themselves been brought up in a tradition which laid great emphasis on parental responsibility for their child's character, they were deeply concerned to do the right thing. While the psychoanalytic writers, in part at least, were concerned with the effects of repression, Truby King later wrote that

> obedience in infancy is the foundation of all later powers of self-control, (King, 1937).

This statement is remarkable for a number of reasons: it indicates how over-ridingly important a particularly Victorian aspect of child behaviour —obedience—was still thought to be as late as 1937; then, by stressing infant obedience, it shows how very little was understood at this time, less than forty years ago, of the infant mind; and it showed too how important was the notion of self-control—an eighteenth century ideal— as an eventual major characteristic of the mature person. The idea that the child was a miniature and potential adult, but not a person in his own right, was still extraordinarily current. Indeed Watson, who in 1928 himself wrote on the psychological care of the infant and child, said that the child should be treated as if he were a young adult! He advocated no hugging or kissing, or any other kind of sentimental interaction with children. At the same time Susan Isaacs was writing that

> if we can really get into our bones . . . the sense of the slow growth of the infant's mind through various bodily experiences and the knowledge that each phase has its own importance in development, we are more likely to give him the gentle and patient friendliness which he most needs . . . (Isaacs, 1929, p. 31).

This is a very different approach from that of Watson and King, yet for two decades at least middle-class parents were subject simultaneously to the influence of both the Behaviourist and the Freudian viewpoints. Newson (1967) quotes reports given by mothers of the time who longed to respond to their babies in a "natural" way, but, possibly because it demanded self-sacrifice and self-control for them not to do this, they considered that they ought, for the child's sake, to be unselfish and adopt the rigorous "Truby King" regime. Freud himself wrote very little about child-rearing, except to stress the need for patience, so that his own influence was an indirect one; but one can say that possibly one of his great contributions to beneficial changes in social attitudes has lain in the effect his discoveries of the processes of development of the infant and child have had on the concept of childhood. His work, coupled with that of such later writers as, for example, Erikson and Piaget, each concerned with different aspects of child development, now make it impossible for us to see childhood as merely a period of preparation of adult life, but enables us to view it as a unique stage in human life, existing in its own right.

However, even the effect of Freudian writers such as Susan Isaacs, was not entirely for good, although she displayed a wisdom and understanding when writing about the infant and young child which was sadly lacking in the writings of the Behaviourists. For example, Isaacs remarked that the only child will be unable to tolerate the least denial of his demands. For this statement and others like it, there was no experimental and, one suspects little, if any, clinical evidence. Further, a misunderstanding of the nature of repression would appear to have been the cause of the cult of permissive rearing, so dominant at one time, particularly in the United States. It is likely that Freud himself would not have approved of this!

What is, on reflection, so depressing about much of the advice given at this time by writers of both schools is that so often dogmatic answers were given to what seems to us now to have been quite irrelevant questions and worries. Of course parents, being anxious to be good parents, have always worried about a child who, for example, is unkind to other children, but many of the worries of parents thirty or forty years ago concerned behaviour of children far too young to understand what was required of them, or the parental anxieties were focused on what we now know to be really non-issues, such as on the apparent importance of early toilet training, or the correct weaning time, or the prevention of thumb sucking (Wood, 1975). On reviewing the history of adult attitudes to children, the most interesting aspect for me lies in observing the move away from seeing children through adult eyes and from the standpoint of adult values, and in place of this notion a move towards understanding the individual child at various phases of his particular childhood. To this end we are at last beginning not to ask irrelevant questions: for example, we no longer ask when to wean and toilet-train, for we know that it is the mother's attitude while handling her baby which really matters. Similarly, child psychologists cannot really advise in a general way whether it is better to discipline firmly or to be permissive: again, the importance lies in the quality of the relationship which exists between parent and child. We now know that the socialization process is not uni-directional, as Bell (1968) and others have pointed out, but that children affect our behaviour as much as we affect theirs; indeed, it is rather charming to reflect on the fact that mothers imitate their babies more than babies imitate their mothers! We also know that the influence we exert on our children is subtle and difficult to identify and to measure.

Now we are no longer concerned to train children primarily to "take their proper place in society", nor, in early childhood at least, to form good habits. However, I do believe that most adults think it important that the children in their care should grow up being able to live happily with other people, respecting their rights and wishes, and also, when mature, to be able to use their gifts and abilities fully (Wood, 1973). We now realize that it is by meeting children's needs at various phases of their development that these aims can best be fulfilled. Kellmer Pringle, 1972), has written that children have four basic needs which are: a need for love and security, for praise and recognition, for responsibility, and for new experiences. And she suggests that it is the ultimate responsibility not only of parents, but of the whole society, through its health, housing and social and educational institutions, to meet these needs.

However, although Kellmer Pringle writes about what we now think we know children need, and how these needs may be met, does this knowledge represent the present-day attitude to children? However much social agencies may try to meet children's needs, the prime responsibility for doing this must in all normal circumstances remain with the parents. In a recent disturbing article in *The Guardian* (16/8/76) Jill Tweedie has expressed concern because a number of changes which have taken place in society during the last two decades or so have detrimentally affected parental interest in, and contact with, their children. The major changes she quotes are: (1) the great increase in the divorce rate; (2) the fact that most mothers now go out to work, and (3) the disruptive effect on family life of television viewing. She writes that a "doleful compromise" is reached between parents and children to the effect that "if you don't bother me, I won't bother you". She says that " 'family' is a grand word for a small flat empty all day and four relative strangers who come together at the end of it for a snatched snack". Far from these conditions enabling parents to exercise the "helping mode", as de Mause suggests is the current fashion, it is possible that a large proportion of our children have seldom been given less help of the kind which is of real importance to them than at the present time. If in due course the structure of the family undergoes radical changes, or even ceases to exist in any recognizable form, what will the social attitudes to children be then?

References

Aries, P. (1962). *Centuries of Childhood*. London: Jonathan Cape.
Bell, R. Q. (1968). A reinterpretation of the direction of effects in studies of socialization. *Psychological Review*, **75**, 81–95.
Cecil, D. (1973). *The Cecils of Hatfield House*. London: Constable and Co.
de Mause, L. L. (1974). *The History of Childhood*. New York: The Psychohistory Press.
Dwight, T. (1955). The father's book. In *Childhood in Contemporary Cultures*. Edited by M. Mead and M. Wolfenstein. Chicago: University of Chicago Press.

Freud, S. (1916). *Introductory Lectures of Psychoanalysis*. Edited by J. Strachey. London: The Hogarth Press and the Institute of Psychoanalysis, 1963.

Gerin, W. (1976). *Elizabeth Gaskell*. Oxford: Oxford University Press.

Isaacs, S. (1929). *The Nursery Years*. London: Routledge and Kegan Paul.

King, F. T. (1937). *Feeding and Care of Baby*. Oxford: Oxford University Press.

Lasareff, V. (1938). *Studies in the Iconography of the Virgin*. Art Bulletin 20. New York.

Mead, M. (1928). *Coming of Age in Samoa*. Harmondsworth, Middx.: Pelican Books.

Newson, E. (1967). Social context and prevailing moralities. *Public Health*, **81,** 176–183.

Newson, J. and Newson, E. (1963). *Infant Care in an Urban Community*. London: Allen and Unwin.

Plumb, J. H. (1975). The new world of children in eighteenth-century England. *Past and Present*, **67,** 64–95.

Pringle, M. L. K. (1972). Address to Chief Police Officers County Councils' Association, London.

Sunley, R. (1955). Early nineteenth-century literature on child rearing. In *Childhood in Contemporary Cultures*. Edited by M. Mead and M. Wolfenstein. Chicago: University of Chicago Press.

Temple, N. (1970). *Seen and Not Heard: A Garland of Fancies for Victorian Children*. London: Hutchinson.

Thompson, P. (1969). Memory and history: report on preliminary interviews. *Social Science Research Council Newsletter*, **6,** 16–18.

Tweedie, J. (1976). Lost youth. *The Guardian*, 16 August.

Wood, M. E. (1973). *Children: The Development of Personality and Behaviour*. London: Harrap and Co.

Wood, M. E. (1975). Cultural Attitude to Child Development. *Concern*, **18,** 7–12.

Some Variations in Marital Satisfaction

CHRISTOPHER WALKER

Department of Social Administration, University of Hull, Hull, England

During the last fifteen years, there have been a number of studies, almost all American, concerned to shed light on the pattern of marital satisfaction over time. Before 1960, interest had focused largely on discovering variables which were correlated with satisfaction, rather than viewing levels of satisfaction as varying over the duration of marriage. There was evidence which suggested a decline in satisfaction, but little was known about the exact nature of the decline or whether it continued throughout the marriage. Studies since then however, have attempted to take into account some notion of passing time, and a little more is now known of the extent to which satisfaction declines and of the pattern of its variation over the marital career.

The impetus for this change has come largely from the work of developmental theorists who were concerned to produce a conceptual framework which would lead to the formulation of family theory. The major full-length treatment of the developmental approach is still that of Duvall (1957), although excellent, if briefer, accounts are given by Hill and Rodgers (1964) and by Rowe (1966). The developmental approach "directs its attention to the longitudinal career of the family system, rather than focusing statically on the family at one point in time", and the major categorization of this longitudinal career has been by means of the family life cycle variable.

The Family Life Cycle

The concept of the life cycle has had a long history, but its starting point as an organized framework for analysing family life stems from the late 1940s. The life cycle defines sequential stages occurring throughout a typical family career, basing the stages on the major developmental tasks being faced by the family. Stages may be based primarily on changes in role and status faced by the marriage partners, for example, that from wife to mother, or the change in occupational status of the husband following retirement; or they may be based on fertility patterns and changes in the development of the children, most importantly, on the age of the oldest child in the family. However, although a variety of classificatory schemes have been developed, including a 24-stage refinement proposed by Rodgers (1962), the most widely used classification is still the eight-stage cycle proposed by Duvall, or minor variations of it. Table I shows the eight stages together with adaptations used in

TABLE I
Delineation of stages in the family life circle

Life cycle stage	Duvall (1957)	British Study	Life cycle stage
I	*Married Couples* (without children)	*Pre-child* (marriage duration less than 5 years, with no children)	I
II	*Childbearing Families* (oldest child birth–30 months)	*Pre-School* (oldest child birth– 5 years	II
III	*Families with Pre-school children* (oldest child 2½–6 years)		
IV	*Families with schoolchildren* (oldest child 6–13 years)	*Primary School* (oldest child 5–12 years	III
V	*Families with Teenagers* (oldest child 13–20 years)	*Secondary School* (oldest child 12–16 years	IV
VI	*Families as Launching Centers* (first child gone to last child's leaving home)	*Launching* (first child's leaving to last child's leaving home, or even if none have left, oldest child is 16 years or older)	V
VII	*Middle-Aged Parents* (empty nest to retirement)		
VIII	*Aging Family Members* (retirement to death of one or both spouses)	*Empty Nest* (empty nest to death of first spouse)	VI

the British study reported later. The effect of these is to collapse the second and third stages into a single pre-school stage and to collapse the last two stages into a single empty-nest stage, while modifying the ages of the oldest child used in the middle stages of the cycle.

Thus far then, there is some consensus in defining the life cycle variable although it is worth bearing in mind right from the start that the life cycle framework has not produced the theoretical gains expected of it. Its utility as an explanatory variable is still open to question, and some of the problems its use poses are discussed later.

Marital Satisfaction

In the measurement of marital satisfaction there is rather more confusion, and certainly more variety. Termed variously satisfaction, success, adjustment or happiness there is still much that is ambiguous both in the concept of marital satisfaction and in the reliability and validity of the scales used to measure it. Three approaches can readily be discerned in the literature, two of which attempt to measure satisfaction with the marriage in general, being scales of greater or lesser complexity, while the third conceives separately the different components of married life and attempts to measure the spouse's satisfaction individually with each of these components.

Thus two composite scales are well known. Blood and Wolfe (1960) combined five components of married life into a single scale. The five components were standard of living, understanding, love, and companionship, together with the congruity of the expected and desired number of children, and the scale was computed by weighting the wife's reported satisfaction with each of these components by the comparative importance she attached to them (Blood, 1967). Similarly, Locke and Wallace (1959) have devised a "short marital-adjustment test" which is again based on the reported satisfaction with eight aspects of married life; though few of these are shared with those used by Blood and Wolfe. It is not immediately obvious that this scale measures simply marital satisfaction, since the test also includes questions on the extent to which the couple share interests, on which partner is dominant in resolving conflicts or disagreements, and on whether or not the spouse would marry the same partner again. But the scale has been widely used as a measure of satisfaction and it is perhaps the only test for which there is reported evidence of reliability (Straus, 1970).

The second approach uses much simpler indices, based often on a single self-rating question. Thus Rollins and Feldman (1970) use a simple six point scale on the question "in general, how often do you think that things between you and your spouse are going well?", with fixed choice responses of "all the time, most of the time, more often than not, occasionally, rarely, or never".

Burr is one of the few writers to have reported findings based on a third approach. In a study of middle-class couples undertaken at the same time as that of Rollins and Feldman, he undertook to distinguish conceptually between satisfaction with six different aspects of the marital relationship, and then to operationalize each of them separately (Burr, 1970).

The areas he selected were the way finances were handled, social activities, performance of household tasks, companionship, sexual interaction and relationships with the children. Despite the differences between these approaches, and the variety of scales used within each approach, it is nevertheless interesting to note some consistency in reported findings, although it is obvious that there is a great deal to be done in improving our conception of marital satisfaction and that much effort is needed to produce successful measurement.

Largely because of the lack of standardized scales and conceptual agreement, the questionnaire used in the British study which was undertaken recently through *Woman's Own* (1974), framed questions in such a way as to permit a variety of approaches to the measurement of satisfaction. The self-report questionnaire included questions asking about the wife's satisfaction with seven components of married life, as well as with her marriage in general "taking it all round". Furthermore, in each of these seven components she was asked not only to rate how satisfied she felt, but how satisfactory she felt her husband was, and how she rated herself or her marriage compared with other wives or marriages of which she knew. Thus data are available for simple indices of general satisfaction, for constructing composite scales, or for analysing the several components separately; and for any or all or these, it is possible to compare or to combine the wife's rating of her marriage, her husband, or how she regards the marriage in comparison with others.

This necessarily brief account of the two variables in question can serve to introduce the American findings, which are placed alongside initial results from the British study.

Findings

At the beginning of the 1960s little was known about the way marital satisfaction varied over the family career. What studies there were suggested a decline although there were some indications of an upward trend in satisfaction towards the later stages of the life cycle. The majority of these and subsequent studies were cross-sectional. The few longitudinal studies did not cover the complete life-cycle career although those that went up to the fifth, teenage, stage were consistent in showing a decline (Pineo, 1961; Paris and Luckey, 1966). Space does not permit a detailed examination of the literature, but two key articles provide at least a starting point for comparison. In 1974, Rollins and Cannon published a re-evaluation of current findings in which they used three different measures of satisfaction. Two measures had been used before with large random samples, but produced conflicting findings. The Blood-Wolfe scale which had been used in 1960 showed a general decline in marital satisfaction over all stages of the life cycle, while the Rollins–Feldman scale in 1970 showed a similar decline in early stages of the cycle but an increase in satisfaction over the later ones. The third measure, the Locke–Wallace test, was included primarily because it had been used in other studies which did not however include the later stages of the cycle.

The patterns reported by Rollins and Cannon are shown in Fig. 1. The scales have been standardized for comparative purposes and mean scores in each stage, which combine responses from husbands and wives, are based on a total sample of some five hundred. All three measures show a decline in satisfaction over the first three stages of the

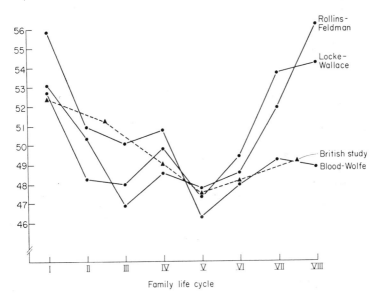

FIG. 1. Mean scores on marital satisfaction by stage of family life cycle.

life cycle, up to and including the pre-school stage, and an increase in satisfaction over the last three, from a low point at the teenage stage through the launching and middle-aged stages to retirement. Again, all three measures show higher levels of satisfaction at Stage IV than at the pre-school and teenage stages on either side. The Locke–Wallace and Rollins–Feldman scales both show a fairly clear U–shape, and both of them indicate reported levels of satisfaction in the aging families stage higher than at the beginning of the life cycle. The Blood–Wolfe scale, although showing increases, has levels of satisfaction at the later stages lower than those reported in the first four.

The pattern of satisfaction found using the general assessment of marriage from the British study is also included in Fig. 1. The scale, which is similar to that of Rollins–Feldman, has raw scores ranging from zero to nine which have been standardized here in the same way as the other three measures (although it covers only the six stage life cycle mentioned earlier). The sample was a self-selected one from readers of *Woman's Own* magazine, and the sample size of 1300 is much larger than in the other studies, giving between one and three hundred cases in all stages of the cycle except the last.

The pattern resembles that from the Blood-Wolfe scale more than those from the other scales, showing a decline up to the secondary school stage (that is, where the oldest child is aged between 12 and 16 years old), and showing an increase over the launching and empty nest stages, although levels of satisfaction here are lower than in the first two stages. Here, as in the American data, there are significant stage differences in mean scores of satisfaction. The findings are thus consistent in showing declining levels of satisfaction from marriage to the stage where the oldest child is of secondary school age, and in showing increasing levels of satisfaction thereafter. They differ in the extent to which satisfaction increases at those later stages, with the Rollins–Cannon and Locke–Wallace scales showing a clear U–shape while the Blood–Wolfe and British data show more of an L–shape.

Before leaving the findings related to measures of general satisfaction, it is perhaps worth pointing out that the collapsing of Duvall's eight-stage cycle into one of six stages does have an effect on the patterns of satsifaction shown. The use of different scales, and of differing scoring procedures, inevitably causes problems of comparison and the literature does not always contain sufficient information about the raw data to facilitate recalculation. But if one takes the mean scores for wives from the Rollins–Feldman measure, and recalculates them combining Stages II and III, and Stages VII and VIII, the effect is to produce a smoother, more symmetrical U–shaped curve, with the combined score in the last, empty-nest, stage slightly lower than in the first stage.

The composite scales so far discussed do combine reported levels of satisfaction on different components of married life, and indeed Rollins and Cannon suggest that the effect of combining the scores simply masks or neutralizes the patterns of satisfaction which differ from component to component. In searching for an explanation of the inconsistent L–shape of the Blood–Wolfe scale they reanalyze the scores on each component part of the scale using a revised weighting system which removes some illogicality in the original calculations. Rollins and Cannon report the illogicality thus:

> for example, if a person is very disappointed with the amount of companionship with his spouse, he gets a higher score on satisfaction with companionship (and thus marital satisfaction) if such companionship is extremely important to him than if he did not value such companionship.

Unfortunately they do not report this secondary analysis in detail, merely suggesting that the patterns of variation on component parts do differ, and that they differ in a way consistent with the findings reported by Burr (1970).

The lowest levels of satisfaction, for each of Burr's six components of married life, occur at his stage three when the oldest child is between 6 and 13 years old. In this his findings are at odds with those of Rollins and Cannon, which showed lower levels of satisfaction at either side of this stage, and with the British study where the lowest levels occurred one stage further on in the cycle when the oldest child was between 12 and 16 years old. Of his separate components, the U–shape was seen most clearly in satisfaction with children and with the way finances are handled in the family. There was less fluctuation over the life-cycle stages with satisfaction in the performance of household tasks and with sexual interaction, and satisfaction with companionship showed a U–shape over the first five of his seven stages but thereafter declined. Burr's sample size was small, and excluded couples from lower socio-economic groupings, but the findings again point to increases in satisfaction over later stages of the family life cycle and certainly suggest that differing patterns will be found when analyzing component areas of married life separately.

The British study included five of Burr's six components and the results confirm variations in patterns of satisfaction dependent on which component is assessed. Satisfaction with companionship, and with understanding in the marriage, display a similar shaped curve to that reporting general satisfaction (shown with a dotted line) although at lower levels throughout every life cycle stage (Fig. 2). The same is true of the wife's satisfaction with the way household tasks are shared, but the curve is flatter at the first and last stages. For these three components, the lowest levels are once again when the oldest child is of secondary school age. A different pattern emerges however when we look at the remaining four components (Fig. 3).

Satisfaction with standard of living is relatively high with little variation over different stages of the life cycle. Overall there is a slight decline, but not such a consistent one as is shown in levels of satisfaction over the way finances are handled in the family. Here the decline is over five of the six stages, with a slight increase in the empty nest stage. The other component which shows a continuous decline is satisfaction with the expression of love and the sexual side of the relationship. Not only is

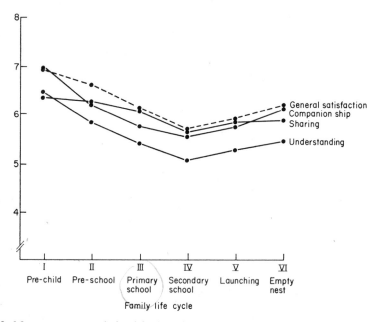

FIG. 2. Mean scores on marital satisfaction with aspects of married life by stage of family life cycle.

the decline continuous throughout all stages, but the mean level of satisfaction is lower for this component of married life than for any of the others. Finally satisfaction with children shows a drop between the pre-school and primary school stages, but is stable thereafter.

Overall the findings suggest that British wives are least satisfied with the expressive components of married life, and the results hold whether the wife is assessing her husband or her marriage. She expects more in the way of companionship, in the amount of understanding of the way she feels and in the expression of love than she presently receives, though she is relatively more satisfied with material aspects of the marriage and with her experiences of motherhood.

Discussion

This examination of some of the findings on variations in marital satisfaction is intended to suggest that the variations which exist are more complex than is revealed by the simple U–shaped curve resulting from plotting mean satisfaction scores over stages of the family life cycle, using some concept of overall satisfaction with the marriage. The more recent articles on the subject display less optimism than earlier ones, with a growing recognition of problems which empirical work had hitherto skirted over, and the following discussion centres on some of these more general problems.

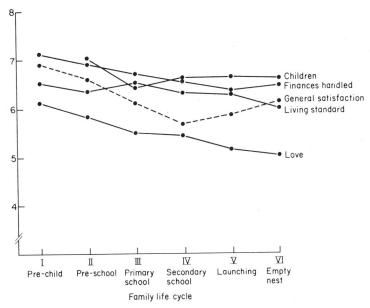

Fig. 3. Mean scores on marital satisfaction with aspects of married life by stage of family life cycle.

There are of course grave problems which arise from the use of cross-sectional, rather than longitudinal data, in attempting to explain variation over time. The practical difficulties in mounting longitudinal research covering complete marriage durations are immediately obvious and, to a certain extent, those studies which have been reported are not greatly at odds with findings from cross-sectional ones. But it remains difficult to disentangle certain factors inherent in cross-sectional studies and this can only cast doubt on some of the inferences so far drawn. For example, in any survey sample taken at a single point in time, those respondents in early stages of the life cycle will be younger and more recently married than those in later stages. It is therefore not easy to discern what generational differences are being reflected in variations in satisfaction over the life cycle. We do not know how far, for example, changes in the level of satisfaction with the sharing of household tasks and responsibilities reflect older traditions of marital roles rather than developmental change in the family. But it is at least plausible to suppose that generational and cohort effects will have an impact on the patterns discovered. To a limited extent only, and providing sample sizes are large, one can begin to control for different ages or for differing marriage durations within stages of the cycle: though some studies have reported difficulties in achieving high response rates, and useable responses, from respondents in later stages of the cycle (Rollins and Cannon, 1974).

Quite another set of problems arise through attrition by marital breakdown. It is known that the majority of breakups which lead to divorce occur in the early stages of the family life cycle (Chester, 1973) when, paradoxically, marital satisfaction is also high. Thus part of the upward trend in levels of satisfaction at later stages may be explained by the absence from the population in all but those early stages of divorcing couples with low satisfaction scores. The position is not as clear as it might be, since there is much still to be discovered about the relationship between marital satisfaction and marital stability: the stable-low satisfaction marriage is one which has so far been relatively neglected. Until more data are available from longitudinal or segmented longitudinal research designs, we can progress only cautiously with the analysis of cross-sectional data; but in doing this we ought perhaps to pay more attention to the life cycle variable itself.

There is first a presentational point which has conceptual implications. Many studies present findings, as is done here, by plotting mean scores of satisfaction for each stage of the life cycle and joining the points by straight lines. Furthermore the life cycle stages are invariably spaced equidistantly along the horizontal axis. This mode of presentation can be extremely misleading. It is all too easy to lose sight of the fact that mean scores are computed from data collected at a single point in time, from sample members who have been categorized into different stages, and not from data collected over the duration of the cycle from sample members as they progress through different stages. And, whilst it is clear that the life cycle is an ordered scale, it is obvious from the way the cycle is defined that the stages are of different durations in time. Sometimes the durations are precisely defined, for example, a couple will spend five years in the pre-school stage, and sometimes less precisely defined, for example, from when the first child leaves home to the empty nest. Moreover the durations can vary from the few months the pregnant bride will spend in stage one, to the several decades which may be spent in the last stage. Thus care needs to be taken both in the interpretation of visual presentations and in the methods of data analysis used.

The idea of processual time in life cycle stages has been discussed at a theoretical level by Rodgers (1962, 1964), and some preliminary attempts have been made at Hull to scale the life cycle variable in terms of processual years rather then in equal intervals. This not only alters the visual appearance of the pattern of satisfaction over time, but it also allows a closer examination of the distribution of scores within a single life cycle stage. The life cycle is presently conceived as marking off distinct developmental stages and it is at least explicitly assumed that there is little variability within each stage. But the initial results from plotting mean scores on satisfaction year by year through life cycle stages shows a very jagged curve, with marked fluctuations not only across, but within stages, and it is not immediately clear that the boundaries of cycle stages mark clear transitional points. Granted the low proportions of variation in satisfaction which are explained by the life cycle variable (nowhere are they reported greater than ten per cent), this adds impetus to those suggesting alternative explanatory schemes, making use, for example, of family events other than fertility to produce a plurality of family careers.

A related point, so far unexplored in the literature, is the likelihood of variations in patterns of marital satisfaction amongst marriages of different circumstances. There is evidence of a relationship between marital satisfaction and a number of other variables, but few studies have investigated the effects of these variables on patterns displayed over the life cycle. Differences between husbands and wives have been explored, since it was believed that they experienced different patterns of satisfaction (Hicks and Platt, 1970), although the more recent studies suggest little significant difference between the patterns. Again, preliminary analysis of the British data suggests that there are variations in the patterns of satisfaction experienced by sub-groups of the sample; for example, between those who rate themselves middle or working-class (working-class respondents showing lower levels of satisfaction throughout and a decline in all but the last stage of the cycle); between respondents marrying at different ages (those marrying under twenty showing earlier decline in satisfaction compared with those marrying when older); between those whose first child was born in the first year of marriage and those whose children were born later (those having a short pre-child stage reporting the lowest satisfaction in the launching, rather than the secondary-school stage); and between those with different family incomes (where those with low-paid husbands report less satisfaction, with very low satisfaction at the secondary school stage). There is clearly much interelatedness between these variables, but much scope for exploring some of the variations in more detail.

In any case the life cycle, even if some standardized form could be agreed, is singularly unsuited to any but the typical pattern of marriage. It does not handle satisfactorily the childless couple, since it makes little sense to maintain couples permanently in the first developmental stage. The usual way round this is simply to exclude couples without children from the analysis after an arbitrary marriage duration though, on the whole, levels of satisfaction are high amongst childless couples. Similarly, there is no obviously satisfactory way to deal with the dissolution of marriage: the data presented here treat only primary marriages but with increasing divorce, and with high rates of remarriage there will be many individuals who leave one life cycle progression and step in, though not necessarily at the same point, to another. If indeed we are to see a greater diversity in marriage patterns, then even as a descriptive device, the utility of the family life cycle variable further declines; leaving us still of course, with the problem of explaining variations in marital satisfaction.

Acknowledgements

My thanks are due to Robert Chester for permission to analyze the British data, which were collected through the agency of *Woman's Own*.

References

Blood, R. O. (1967). *Love Match and Arranged Marriage: A Tokyo-Detroit Comparison.* New York: Free Press.

Blood, R. O. and Wolfe, D. M. (1960). *Husbands and Wives: The Dynamics of Married Living.* Glencoe, Illinois: Free Press.

Burr, W. R. (1970). Satisfaction with various aspects of marriage over the life cycle: a random middle-class sample. *Journal of Marriage and the Family,* **32,** 29–37.

Chester, R. (1973). *Divorce and the Family Life Cycle in Great Britain.* Paper presented to the Thirteenth Annual Seminar of the Committee on Family Research of the International Sociological Association. Paris.

Duvall, E. M. (1957). *Family Development.* Revised Ed. 1962. Philadelphia: Lippincott.

Hicks, M. W. and Platt, M. (1970). Marital happiness and stability: a review of the research of the sixties. *Journal of Marriage and the Family,* **32,** 553–574.

Hill, R. and Rodgers, R. H. (1964). The developmental approach. In *Handbook of Marriage and the Family.* Edited by H. T. Christensen. Chicago: Rand McNally.

Locke, H. J. and Wallace, K. M. (1959). Short marital adjustment and prediction tests: their reliability and validity. *Marriage and Family Living,* **21,** 251–255.

Paris, B. L. and Luckey, E. B. (1966). A longitudinal study of marital satisfaction. *Sociology and Social Research,* **30,** 212–223.

Pineo, P. E. (1961). Disenchantment in the later years of marriage. *Marriage and Family Living,* **23,** 3–11.

Rodgers, R. H. (1962). *Improvements in the Construction and Analysis of Family Life Cycle Categories.* Kalamazoo: Western Michigan University.

Rodgers, R. H. (1964). Towards a theory of family development. *Journal of Marriage and the Family,* **26,** 262–270.

Rollins, B. C. and Cannon, K. L. (1974). Marital satisfaction over the family life cycle: a reevaluation. *Journal of Marriage and the Family,* **36,** 271–282.

Rollins, B. C. and Feldman, H. (1970). Marital satisfaction over the family life cycle. *Journal of Marriage and the Family,* **32** ,20–28.

Rowe, G. P. (1966). The developmental conceptual framework to the study of the family. In *Emerging Conceptual Frameworks in Family Analysis.* Edited by F. I. Nye and F. M. Berardo. New York: Macmillan.

Straus, M. (1970). *Family Measurement Techniques.* Chicago: Rand McNally.

Woman's Own (1974). A Questionnaire. 12 October.

Sexuality in Old Age

ALEX COMFORT

Institute for Higher Studies, Santa Barbara, California, USA

Aging induces some changes in human sexual performance. These are chiefly in the male, where orgasm becomes less frequent and where more direct physical stimulation is required to produce erection; but compared with age changes in other fields such as muscular strength or vital capacity these changes are functionally minimal. Sexuality, in other words, lasts in humans of both sexes much better than most or many other functional systems. In fact, in the absence of disease, sexual requirement and capacity are lifelong, and even if and when actual intercourse fails through infirmity the need for other aspects of sexual relationship such as closeness, sensuality and being valued persist. This is totally contrary to folklore and to the preconceptions of hospital and nursing home administrators, some of whom seem to dislike sexuality even among staff. It is even contrary to the beliefs of many older people themselves—they have been in a sense hocussed out of continuing sexual activity by a society which disallowed it for the old, exactly as they have been hocussed out of so many other valuable activities of which they are fully capable such as useful work, social involvement (in the name of disengagement) and even continued life, through being wished away by well-meaning relatives. You recall Tom Lehrer, "In all probability I'll lose my virility—and you your fertility and desirability" . . . The odd thing is that the hocussing has not been more successful. We have remarked elsewhere that in our experience old folks stop having sex for the same reasons they stop riding a bicycle, i.e. general infirmity, thinking it looks ridiculous, and no bicycle. Of these the greatest is the social image of the dirty old man and the asexual, undesirable older woman. We have been dealing with aging in what has been very much a sexually handicapped society.

As in so many other sexual contexts, the handicap has been self-renewing and self-maintaining until lately. Old people were not asked about sexual activity because they were assumed to have none, and assumed to have none because they were not asked. Such questions were excluded from histories because they might cause embarrassment, and they continued to cause embarrassment (though much less to the patient than the doctor) because they were not normally included. Our fantasy of the asexual senior when we are younger becomes a blueprint for our own aging when we get older, and is a classical process of bewitchment by social expectation.

In fact, as Simone de Beauvoir (1972) pointed out, the facts were there all along, as they were over other sexual matters such as the normality of masturbation, but they had undergone the invisibility usual to facts which do not fit a social preconception.

Statistical studies on the sexual activity of old people are instructive as they tend to show that old people have always been sexually active, but that this activity has been reinforced as the attitude of the culture has become less negative. We need to bear in mind that those now aged 80 had the sexual indoctrination of the year 1905. In America that was pretty varied as between New England and, say, New Orleans, and the differences between what the Japanese call the "front" and the "back" cultures were great. As far back as 1926 Raymond Pearl recorded that nearly 4 per cent of males between 70–79 having intercourse every third day and nearly 9 per cent more were having it weekly (Pearl, 1930). Kinsey's figures pointed to a decline in coital frequency in both sexes with age, but these figures were cross-sectional. In 1959 Finkle and his co-workers questioned 101 men aged 56 to 86, ambulant patients with no complaint likely to affect potency, and found 65 per cent under age 69 and 34 per cent over 70 still potent, with two out of five over 80 averaging ten copulations a year. When investigated further they found that some in the sample had never had intercourse. Others, though potent, had no partner. In the over-70 group the main reason given for sexual inactivity was "no desire" and, of all the men over 65, only three gave as reason "no erection". Newman and Nichols (1960) questioned men and women from 60 to 93 years of age and found 54 per cent active overall. No significant decline was found under 75. Among those over 75, 25 per cent were still active and the fall was accounted for chiefly by illness of self or spouse.

> Those who rated sexual urges as strongest in youth rated them as moderate in old age: most who described sexual feelings as weak to moderate in youth described themselves as without sexual feelings in old age.

confirming Pearl's 1926 finding that early starters are late finishers. Pfeiffer *et al.* (1968) at Duke University studied 254 people of both sexes and found that the median age for stopping "sexual activity" (presumably coitus, not masturbation) was 68 in men, range 49–90, and 60 in women with a high record of 81, the difference being due to the age differential (average four years) between spouses. The figures for regular and frequent intercourse were 47 per cent between 60 and 71 and 15 per cent age 78 and over. The most interesting part of this study is that unlike previous examinations it was longitudinal not cross-sectional. Over a five-year period 16 per cent of propositi reported a falling off of activity but 14 per cent reported an increase. What we are seeing in cross-sectional studies, therefore, is a mixture of high and low sexually-active individuals, in which those whose sexual "set" is low for physical or attitudinal reasons drop out early—often using age as a justification for laying down what has for them been an anxious business. Social pressure, ill health and the ill health of a partner, and lack of a partner take some toll among the others, but among the sexually active and sexually unanxious when young, aging abolishes neither the need, nor the capacity for intercourse. A generation which has lived sexually, viewed sexual activity positively and has aged, not in the expectation of asexuality and impotence but of continuing as long as possible in the style they have known, will quite certainly sample very much higher than the propositi in these studies. Today, individual variation is large, continuance of sex activity depends on the set and the life-pattern of each patient, and older people experience the changes in normal sexual physiology which I have described, but that is all. The negative picture is folklore; part of the negative folklore of aging, it is self-fulfilling, and it is preventable if we set the record straight.

Bearing in mind that these figures include those whose sex lives were never vigorous, or who laid down sexuality willingly as an embarrassing burden, those still active are probably sexually unanxious people whose valuation of sexuality has run counter to society's constant attempts at castration.

Exactly the same has happened, incidentally, over performance and intelligence with age. Preconceived ideas have realized themselves, helped by confusion between longitudinal and cross-sectional work, and between aging and age-linked pathologies such as atherosclerosis. It has taken the careful work of Eisdorfer and others to show how little is the age-decline in performance intrinsic and how much it depends on self-fulfilling prophecy. So long as we treat the old as asexual, ineducable, unemployable and unintelligent some of them will oblige by being so. The next "old", however, will not. They, incidentally, will be us and I doubt if we shall let society impose on us the patterns it imposed on our grandfathers.

Bering in mind that people who are now 80 were born in 1897, I think we can anticipate that our, and future generations, whose valuation of sexuality is higher and whose anxieties about it are less, will go much less gently into that good night, a fact which nursing home administrators must take to heart.

For those who are old now, sexuality, if it can be maintained, or revived without impertinent interference, or at least not condemned, mocked or obstructed, is a solace, a continued source of self-value, and a preservative. Not all will wish to have it pressed upon them, but at least we could stop turning it off. Surgeons could stop doing radical prostatic and other pelvic operations which compromise potency on the assumption that after sixty it will not be needed, or suggesting that for certain conditions the vagina of elderly women should simply be sewn up. The idea of providing petting rooms in hospitals is well-meaning but is part of the patronizing view of the old which we would not much like if it were offered to us. They need not petting but privacy. We have to impress this on society, despite its Freudian anxieties about parental intercourse, that all humans are sexual beings retaining the same needs until they die. If we can do it without applying evangelistic pressures, we have to get it through the head of the old and the aging that loving and being loved, both in their full physical expression, are never inaesthetic nor contemptible if they are appropriate. To quote Richard Burton:

> Ancient Men will dote in this kind sometimes as well as the rest; the heat of love will thaw their frozen Affections, dissolve the ice of age, and so enable them, though they be three score Years of age above the girdle, to be scarce thirty beneath. (*It is interesting that for Burton, a man of sixty, is considered aged.*) Otherwise it is most odious, when an old Acherontick Dizard, that hath one foot in his Grave, shall flicker after a lusty wench . . .

Even Burton was clearly not fully aware of the active sexuality of the old. Few authors, indeed, have been until our own day; the old were aware of it, if one asked them, but kept their own counsel for fear of hostile comment. Burton's traditional view is easier for men to accept. It has been cruelly remarked that women have a menopause, but men do not have a womenopause. Now women are as conscious of their needs and their capacity as are men, but they fear rejection and the state of being not desired or not desirable. They have not been helped by the social image of competition for youth, but I think this situation will change. It will change because our valuation of sexuality is changing, and because of the growing number of older people. I do not believe that the movies of twenty years from now will all be about *young* lovers. Many are going to be about older lovers. There will be an interregnum when promotion switches to the middle-aged, an interregnum of plastic surgery and rejuvenation exploitation, but I also think that this will pass. The remedy for it lies in an increasing social awareness of the falsity of the sex-object game which women have been induced to play, and have sometimes played willingly, and the growing acceptance of people as people, the rise of the elders which my colleague Harvey Wheeler at the Institute for Higher Studies, has described. I think the demographic shortage of women in some cohorts will help, even though the traditional male expedient is to raid younger age groups for mates. In fact I think we would agree that really experienced males are happy to have intercourse with a woman of any age who experiences herself as a fully sexual person.

It is important, especially in view of the creation of "postmature ejaculation" or "ejaculatory incapacity" as a label, to explain to older males that they will probably not ejaculate vaginally at every act if intercourse is frequent. Ejaculation can usually be produced by masturbation if desired, but frequent masturbation at this time may reduce sensitivity. The slower response of older men can be seen as an improvement of function, given the short coital times reported at earlier ages.

A related syndrome is seen in older couples when the post-menopausal woman is put on hormone maintenance therapy. In this case lubrication may be greatly increased, the male cannot reach orgasm, and fears he is becoming impotent. Explanation and dose adjustment are indicated.

Sexual activity prolongs life in rats. There is no hard evidence that it does so in people. It would however be very interesting to compare the sexual frequencies reported by coronary and matched non-coronary males in the late 50s, on the basis that short bursts of tachycardia such as those experienced during coitus have been recommended by some exercise physiologists as a protective against heart attack. The role of sexual activity and sexual frustration in producing or preventing prostatic disease has also never been investigated. With a decrease in patient reticence and doctor embarrassment, such studies are now possible.

The value of hormone supplements in women has been much debated. In men, they may lower orgasmic threshold, but the main action of androgens seems to be in improving well-being and hence response generally. Mesterolone is probably the agent of choice, since it is not "read" by the hypothalamus as testosterone, and administration does not cut off endogenous androgen production. Androgen levels in age vary, and are only rarely deficient.

My general conclusions are these. Geriatricians need to support and encourage the sexuality of the old without embarrassing or evangelizing them. It is a mental, social, and probably a physical, preservative of their status as persons, which our society already attacks in so many cruel ways. Abram Maslow stressed long ago the relation of sexual activity to dominance and to peak experiences: it has a function in ego-preservation. We can at least stop mocking, governessing and segregating the old and the aging: it is to their sexuality, after all, that we owe our own existence, and that sexuality is honorable. Generations which have grown up with full and unanxious sex lives are not going to drop them at the whim of a nursing-home administrator or at an arbitrary chronological age.

How far the sexuality of the old can be rekindled or encouraged depends on them, and their wishes and feelings, but as with the disabled, who have been similarly victims of black social magic, we can do a lot by non-discouragement. This includes the avoidance of medical, surgical or social castration. Early counselling is needed to neutralize the jinx which faces many people as they age as is research into, and repetition of, the facts about continued male potency and female capacity. In some cases active therapy with hormones, decent and judicious cosmetic surgery, and counselling will also be necessary. Old men need to be warned of the risk of "sexual disuse atrophy" rather as they are warned against bed rest. Obesity is a common cause of impotence. Alcohol is a powerful sedative and quite a usual contributor to impotence at all ages. Slightly younger men need information about the normal decline in orgasm frequency; they should be encouraged to enjoy the extra mileage, and their partners briefed about the need for more direct tactile stimulation. Older people seem to profit from instruction in cultivating some of the gentler and less specifically genital forms of sensuality and sexual expression, and are often very ready for them. If their sex lives have been full and their sensuality not blocked by anxiety or convention, sexuality in old age becomes a different and a quieter experience but not less sexual and no less an experience than in youth. Nor is it ever too late to learn; one hears of anorgasmic women who in their late 60s or even their 70s have learned to masturbate and then to progress to coital orgasm for the first time in their lives. Their motive in coming for treatment was that they did not want to die without the full experience of womanhood. As to the fear of rejection by each other, or by others, as ridiculous or oversexed, anyone who has watched many people making love (and very few sex pundits have) would agree that people of all ages look more beautiful and less absurd doing that than doing almost anything else, such as playing golf. There are many simple, procedures which can help. for example, conservative prostatic surgery, treatment of prolapse and senile vaginitis, correction of pendulous breasts and other minor gynaecological problems and treatment for depression, diabetes, obesity, and alcoholism.

Some drugs like DOET, which alter the backdrop of consciousness, may also be of use, but we can probably help most by not hindering, and not letting others hinder, the normal continuance of a normal and necessary function which stays fully effective in its relational and recreational uses, and statistically its main uses in humans, long after its reproductive functions are over. Most people can and should expect to have sex long after they no longer wish to ride bicycles. Such people need fewer tranquillizers, less institutionalization, and live richer lives.

I have said we need to help without impertinent interference. In the case of the disabled we were always told that reference to their sex needs could embarrass them, in fact; when counselling was offered, they beat a path to the door. I suspect the same would happen with the old. Some of that counselling will come from the regular physician, but he may not always have the requisite sexual know-how. Quite a feasible arrangement is that sexuality be allowed or gently encouraged to come up in group discussion among couples, and that can move on to more individual sensuality training of the same kind which helps some people of any age. The fact of peer discussion alone is a reassurance and a help to very many people; not infrequently when it has become really frank and any initial embarrassments have been overcome, people solve each other's problems. This is certainly true of the disabled and I expect it would be true of the old. Discussion also serves to create a climate of renewed sexual interest and hope which can quite transform the atmosphere of a home for the disabled, and could, I think, do so even more for a retirement home where people are not disabled, only very often discouraged. What the institutional old require is not the provision of petting rooms, but the privacy and autonomy which other adults enjoy in choosing or rejecting sexual options. The wish to exercise that option is not evidence of senility, and its exercise is worth more than medication in re-establishing and maintaining the sense of self. A really good book on sex for the older citizen could be a big start as a nonsense-corrective. It is rather nice that many older people have been resexualized or even fully sexualized for the first time, by aware sons and daughters. This service for them in the recreational and relational use of sex compensates in part for the service they did us in its reproductive use.

References

de Beauvoir, S. (1972). *Old Age*. New York: Putnam.

Finkle, A. L., Moyers, T. G., Tobenkin, M. I. and Karg, S. J. (1959). Sexual potency in aging males. I. Frequency of coitus among clinic patients. *Journal of the Amercian Medical Association*, **170,** 1391–1393.

Newman, G. and Nichols, C. R. (1960). Sexual activities and attitudes in older persons. *Journal of the American Medical Association*, **173,** 33–35.

Pearl, R. (1930). *The Biology of Population Growth*. New York: Knopf.

Pfeiffer, E., Werwoerdt, A. and Wang, H. S. (1968). Sexual behaviour in aged men and women. *Archives of General Psychiatry*, **19,** 753–758.

The One-Parent Family: Deviant or Variant?

ROBERT CHESTER

Department of Social Administration, The University of Hull, Hull, England

Introduction

When study is made of diversity in family structures the context is usually either that of cross-cultural differences, or of intra-cultural variations exhibited by segments of a population such as social classes or urban and rural communities. Within this mould of family study attention has been specifically given to a single-parent form of family structure, as for instance the matri-centred families of some Caribbean areas and American ghettoes, where this feature is held to be culture-related if not culturally determined. Increasingly in developed societies, however, it has become necessary to give attention to single-parent forms of the family which spring from variations in biographical circumstance rather than from the cultural characteristics of groups. One-parent families have become sufficiently familiar to be both socially and sociologically significant, so that Cockburn and Heclo (1974) were able to conclude from their review of European data that

> the proportion of single-parent families in the countries surveyed is approximately of the same order of magnitude as the proportion in Britain (with its 9 per cent of all families with dependent children).

Although different segments of the population may have differential propensity to produce one-parent families, these families are not characteristic of the group, and neither do they arise from principled rejection of the ideologically orthodox and statistically normal two-parent form. They arise, rather, from individual circumstances such as unmarried motherhood, widowhood, divorce and separation, and in many cases marriage or remarriage produce orthodox two-parent families in due course, but two points should be noted. First, the periods which individual families spend in one-parent circumstances are in general sufficiently lengthy to ensure that the experience forms a significant fraction of the lives of family members, and particularly of the phase of dependent childhood. Secondly, the turnover in membership of the category ensures that the cumulative incidence of the experience is much greater than its current prevalence of some 10 per cent. A large minority of the population may come to experience the single-parent condition at some point in their lives, in some cases both as children and as parents themselves, so that it is important to consider the viability of this family form in contemporary social conditions.

Single-parent Families
Single-parent families vary among themselves both in composition and in the circumstances of their formation, and these variations are relevant to the kind of experience which members have. The family may be headed by either a mother or a father, for instance, and children may be at different developmental stages. Some have only one adult present from their formation, while others experience the loss of a parent through death or through the formal or informal break-up of the marriage. As the Finer Committee found, quantification in this sphere is difficult, especially where interest is in distinctive domestic situations rather than in the procedural categories of official enumerators, but there is no doubt that broken marriage currently exceeds both death and unmarried motherhood combined as a cause of single-parenthood, with divorce in particular making an increasing contribution. Unfortunately, the categories of divorced and separated are not fully discrete. Most of those who divorce are separated first, with or without legal sanction, while many (and now perhaps most) of those currently separated will eventually divorce, although some will remain simply separated and others will effect reconciliations. The permanent ending of marriage can be recognized only retrospectively, but analytically it is possible to focus upon those whose break-up transpires to be final, and the intention here is to concentrate primarily upon one-parent families created in this way. Apart from the fact that they are in the majority, such one-parent families have features which distinguish them from others, and they are in a sense particularly characteristic of the times. Not all studies differentiate among types of one-parent family by cause, however, and so reference will be made to material which includes all types.

Within this focus upon one-parent families created by disruption of marriage there will further be concentration on those which are headed by the mother, because these are particularly likely to experience certain deprivations, and because they are in the great majority. Again quantification is difficult, but there are various clues in the literature to the sex differential involved. In the National Child Development Study 9·4 per cent of children had lost one parent and remained with the other by age eleven, and the ratio of father loss to mother loss was about $4\frac{1}{2}$:1 (Ferri, 1973). This compares with just under 4:1 in the 1966 Census, and just 4:1 among primary school children studied for the *Plowden Report* (1967). Women may therefore be about four times as likely as men to find themselves heading one-parent families, but there are two points to make on this. Firstly, the ratio is affected by the age of the children concerned. The NCDS study of children at age seven showed fatherless children outnumbered motherless by about 6:1, while Rowntree (1955) found 7:1 among children aged four in the National Study of Health and Development, so that women are particularly apt to find themselves caring single-handed for children who are in the younger and thus more dependent groups. The second point is that the sex ratio among lone parents is also affected by the cause of the situation. Of the NCDS children whose situation was caused by break-up of marriage, 84 per cent were left with the mother against only 71 per cent where parental death was the cause. And confirming both these points, Rowntree found mothers caring for 96 per cent of the four-year-olds in the cases of broken marriage, against 73 per cent where a parent had died. It seems probable, therefore, that when marriage involving minor children break up the wife is some four or five times more likely to be left with the children, with an even greater differential where younger children are concerned. For this reason most of the issues which follow are examined by reference to female-headed families where break-up of marriage is responsible for the situation.

Stigma and Social Ambiguity

What are the attitudes towards such families? There is no doubt that at the popular level they are regarded as deviant twice over; deviant because only one parent is present, and deviant again because the head of the household is a woman. In England, at least, these families are stigmatized, and the role of divorced or separated wife is dishonoured and socially invalid (Chester and Streather, 1972; Hart, 1976). Such women are commonly seen as ones who have failed in their sex roles (by not keeping their man), and are often thought to be immature, irresponsible or neurotic. Their children are expected to be undisciplined, possibly delinquent, suffering from sex role confusion and vulnerable to many pathologies. Cultural stereotypes foster beliefs that such women are both sexually needy and sexually predatory, and so they tend to experience offensive sexual overtures from men and wariness or hostility from women. Furthermore, they undergo sexual surveillance not only by social peers, but also by public officials, since when social security support is required the state substitutes for the absent husband in regulating various of the woman's activities. Female-headed families thus lack good social credentials, and many of the women internalize social attitudes so that they feel shame and insecurity. Social relationships are often marked by mutual embarrassments which give rise to withdrawal or exclusion from sociability.

Stigmatization of one-parent families, however, is not restricted to popular social circles but is seen also in taken-for-granted assumptions commonly found in the professional literature. In sociology the most prominent theoretical perspectives in the study of the family can be grouped under the general label "functionalist", and within this the ideas of Talcott Parsons on the structure and functioning of the nuclear family have been especially influential. Of particular relevance here is the distinction which Parsons makes between instrumental and expressive roles, and the way these are linked by him to the two sexes. Instrumental roles (concerned with goal attainment, adaptation, etc.) are ascribed to the male, and expressive roles (integration and nurture) to the female, so that a "properly-constituted" family requires two parents. It is not intended here to dismiss functionalist perspection on the family, or even to argue with them in any detail, but as Morgan (1975) has pointed out, the functionalist emphasis can have several untoward aspects. Among these are tendencies to a static or a historical approach; to over-systematization; to reification; to the generation of a notion of a proper constellation of family roles; and in general, to an emphasis upon constraints rather than on potentialities in human action. The conservatizing tendency in functionalist thought is shared by some other sociological approaches to the family, such as the developmental or family life cycle perspective. The family life cycle is conceived as a progression of changes which may routinely be expected to occur over time in the size, age-composition and role-structure of an elementary family. As a heuristic tool it is unobjectionable, but the notion of the cycle can subtly become coercive both intellectually and normatively, so that departures from the standard developmental pathway come to be called deviations rather than variations (Turner, 1969).

One consequence of such theoretical orientations, together with uncritically-imported commonsense cultural assumptions about the family, is a common research presumption of pathology, so that rather than being regarded as alternative and potentially viable family forms single-parent families are termed "broken", "incomplete", "dis-organized", etc. Divorce and separation are sometimes referred to as *family* dissolution, and the term "broken home" is often used in somewhat sentimental fashion, although strictly speaking divorce represents the dissolution of the *marriage* rather than of the family, which is not so much broken or dissolved as reorganized with the departure of one member. This professional attitude may be summarized with a question from a well-known text on sociology and medicine, which runs, "We can anticipate characteristic difficulties, social, psychological and medical, among such *dysmorphic* families" (Susser and Watson, 1971; stress not in the original). Characteristic difficulties indeed there are, but it is important to consider how far these are inherent or unavoidably present in one-parent families, and how far they represent instead the outcome of society's failure to provide for the consequences of terminated marriage and its reluctance to endorse any family form other than that which is ideologically prescribed.

Adverse stereotypes have been noted, but the roles concerned are not only stigmatized, they are also ambiguous. In his analysis of the discomforts of divorced status and pressures to remarry, Goode (1965), gives great emphasis to this factor, but it is possible to dissent from the emphasis which he gives to institutional ambiguity while conceding that it does exist and is significant. The statuses of "estranged spouse" and "divorcee" are socially deprecated, as noted above, and consequently there is little institutional regulation of the behaviour of the spouses (and relevant others) either during the break-up process or afterwards. Specifically, there is no *particular* ethical guidance about the provision of emotional or material support (unlike the case of widowhood), and no rule concerning re-admission to former kin groups, or on the attitudes which kin should take to remarriage. There is no clear specification of how the ex-spouses should relate to each other, how they should feel, how they should behave in heterosexual encounters, etc. Being formerly-married, that is to say, is not at all the same thing as being unmarried, and institutional lacunae produce individual discomfort. This uncomfortable ambiguity is shared by both sexes, but is compounded for the woman by the bearing of her husband's surname and the style "Mrs". These features symbolically affirm that she has left her natal group and emphasize her ambiguous position, but if she has children reversion to her maiden style and name carries the risk that she will be thought an unmarried mother. Both sexes must cope with the status-incongruity of being non-married parents, but for men this is partly offset by the fact that they typically spend more time in spheres (such as work) where interaction is less governed by marital and parental status. More frequent interaction in neighbourhood and community settings may present women with greater problems of information control.

Respondents in studies of the divorced and separated undoubtedly manifest a sense of status ambiguity (George and Wilding, 1972; Marsden, 1973; Hart, 1976). They describe social situations where they felt unsure how to behave, and similar uncertainty on the part of others, both kinds of experience often leading to withdrawal or exclusion. Because of normative haziness they sometimes felt that they could be criticized whatever they did, and there is no reason to doubt the penalizing significance of status ambiguity and absence of role prescription. It is reasonable, however, to doubt the primacy which is accorded to these by Goode, because it is doubtful that consensus and clear role-specification are the general rule for the other statuses. Like many role theorists, he perhaps takes a somewhat over-determined view of the role-structure of society and exaggerates the degree of clarity of role-definition in a changeful world. There is much argument on conjugal roles, for instance, and indeed some marriages break up because of role dissensus. Roles of many kinds are more indeterminate and negotiable than is implied in Goode's stress on status ambiguity, and of course he himself recognizes other sources of discomfort. It is likely that the social discomposure of single parents follows at least as much from stigmatization as from normative mystification, and it is certain that the two together constitute a source of social exclusion, so that members of one-parent families have problems of reputation, self-validation and the negotiation of a legitimate social identity. These matters, however, are not the only ones which incommode such families, and it is necessary to recognize other effective sources of deprivation and discomfort which arise from the cumulative press of the normal working of socially-structured arrangements.

Structural Pressures

After the departure of one parent there are three analytically distinct possibilities open to the remaining family members (although two or more may be adopted in sequence).

(i) They may disband as a separate unit (for instance by the children going into public care or by members becoming absorbed into another domestic unit). By definition, one-parent families have not taken this route.

(ii) There can be redistribution of role responsibilities, which can be reorganized and re-allocated among remaining members (with or without some loss of function). This is the option which produces one-parent families.

(iii) There can be reconstitution through the incorporation of a newcomer to take over all or some of the functions of the missing member. Typically this means remarriage, although informal cohabitation is another possibility.

For those adopting option (ii) certain difficulties arise from the nature of social and economic arrangements, and here it is intended to examine very briefly the areas of economic support, domestic responsibilities, and access to sociability and emotionally-supportive relationships. The contention will be that problems arising in these spheres, together with the status-ambiguity and stigma already noted, constitute latent but very strong pressures towards the adoption of option (iii)—reconstitution—and that many of the "characteristic difficulties" found among one-parent families may spring not from the inherent nature of the situation but from the social response to it.

ECONOMIC SUPPORT

The family must get an income, and for all practical purposes this means that the lone parent must either work or claim social security benefits. It is true that some women are entitled to maintenance, but this rarely obviates the need for state benefits and often simply involves the woman in stress and indignity through non-payment. Lone fathers typically have full-time jobs at break-up, and can retain them if willing and able to find domestic assistance (although stress frequently reduces their work-capacity). Sex differences in job opportunity, qualifications and pay mean that the financial advantages of working are more considerable for men than for women, although by working part time the latter may supplement social security benefits to a minor degree. According to George and Wilding there is normative pressure for men to work rather than to remain at home on state benefits, and only 19 per cent of their sample of lone fathers chose the latter course (some of whom were anyway ineligible to work). Public opinion evidently sees work as important to the integrity, identity and self-respect of men, and the men's own internalized values supported this view. The public also believe that lone mothers with *older* children should work, although this belief is differently based. Part-time work is favoured, and is favoured more for the woman's own benefit than for getting her off social security. Maternal obligations seem to over-ride economic obligations more than do paternal, and women can find more normative support in claiming public funds. In consequence of all this, most estranged or divorced lone fathers work, and most corresponding mothers draw benefits and possibly work part time. Divorce and separation, therefore, do not characteristically lead to the reversal of traditional economic roles, but this has implications for income (Hunt, 1973).

Generalization is difficult, but there appears to be a hierarchy of income running down from two-parent through mother-absent to father-absent families. According to Hunt, when adjusted for family size the mean incomes of lone fathers run at about one-third less than those of two-parent families, probably reflecting the absence of a wife's wage, family-imposed restrictions on overtime etc. The incomes of lone mothers, however, average only some two-thirds of those of lone fathers, and in Hunt's terminology at least three-quarters of such women were classified as "low income". *The Report of the Committee on One-parent Families* (1974) summarizing much of the available information, leaves no doubt at all that female-headed families are apt to be poor. Furthermore, there seems to be a hierarchy among such families, with widows having more income than divorced or separated wives, who in turn have more than unmarried mothers, and this pattern probably symbolizes social evaluation of these categories. The evidence further suggests that female-headed families are deficient not only in income but also in household capital in the form of domestic amenities and appliances. To some extent this may reflect standard of living during marriage, but it also reflects inability on subsistence income to undertake maintenance or replacement of houshold items, and low income naturally also carries implications for dietary levels, clothing etc. Certainly it can be stated that economic deprivation is normal for female-headed one-parent families, and clearly this undermines the viability of the family form.

DOMESTIC RESPONSIBILITIES

Single-handed management and servicing of a household create problems of time and energy allocation which for those who work may be particularly severe, and possible consequences are household neglect or personal overstrain. Whether the lone parent is employed or not, however, child care and socialization often present problems. Parenting contains both instrumental and expressive elements which are conventionally divided on a sex-linked basis. The evidence suggests that many people find difficulty with combining in themselves, on a continuing basis, both the emotional nurturance and the authority/discipline aspects of child-rearing. George and Wilding reported that fathers tended to be anxious about coping with children's emotional needs, while Marsden found that in more than one-third of cases mothers were barely in control of their children, with anarchy sometimes reigning, and this accords with social assumptions about indiscipline. In two-parent families the adults offer each other relief and mediation in dealings with children, besides the emotional sustenance that comes from relationships with peers, and the absence of these things makes for frustration and fatigue. Children may also suffer in these circumstances because the parental behaviour they experience may be inconsistent, indecisive, or unduly rigid.

Social welfare agencies have seemed so far unable or unwilling to provide facilities or support related to parental functions. This is an area in which research and experimental provision would be valuable, but there is a subtle issue here which tends to be ignored. Much of the relevant research has tended to focus upon father-loss and paternal deprivation (and has also tended to emphasize the consequences for boys, on the possibly false assumption that they are more seriously affected by the absence of a male figure). However, if mothers are habitually physically or emotionally overstrained by their responsibilities and if furthermore they are trying to play some part of "the father's role" in childrearing, then in a paradoxical way the children may in fact suffer from *maternal* deprivation. The interactional processes of one-parent families are probably quite complicated, and in studies of father-absent families it is clearly necessary to allow for the implications of single-handed parenthood for the mother's behaviour. Father-absent families, that is to say, are not just like father-present families with the father removed, and research design has to cater for this.

It is certainly clear that some of the taxing nature of solo parenthood and household management reflects the absence of community-provided supports but lone mothers have a further authority problem, and this is in relation to the gatekeeping function of heads of households. The head of a household mediates between the family and community agencies, and in this two-way representation a female head is handicapped by the fact that women in general have less standing and power than men. Since she is perceived as playing a deviant role anyway, such a woman is likely to be at a disadvantage and the family may experience a general loss of power *vis-a-vis* the outside world and the general institutions of society. In interviews such women have complained of difficulties regarding credit, dealing with officials and workmen, etc., and have spoken of a general sense of being put upon, of vulnerability, and loss of community standing. In various ways, therefore, it is clear that the assumptions structured into community institutions and agency attitudes make life difficult for lone mothers.

SOCIABILITY AND SOCIAL SUPPORT

Adult social life in most British communities is oriented towards couples. Patterns of invitation and response, topics of conversation, and systems of co-operation revolve around couples and their concerns, and there is little place for the unaccompanied in the structure of sociability. It is true that some isolation is self-imposed through feelings of self-doubt and sensitivity to slight, and true also that lone parents find special difficulty in getting out socially because of burdensome obligations, problems of child care, and lack of finance. The last factor has special relevance for women in relation to commercially-based sociability, but in any case contemporary mores place more restrictions on public social ventures for unaccompanied women than for men (Garvey, 1974). Lone parents are socially anomalous and are aware of this, and thus in another way they find themselves excluded. Loneliness is a common experience for both sexes, sometimes to an extreme degree. Clubs for the divorced and separated are reflections of the difficulties encountered in finding sociable outlets, but such clubs are few and their segregationist tendencies are not congenial to all (Hart, 1976). Women in particular thus tend to be cut off not only from emotionally-supportive adult companionship but also from networks of communication regarding local news, offers and opportunities. The most straightforward way of countering all this exclusion is to find a permanent partner, and thus an entry ticket to orthodox society and sociability.

Conclusion

It can be seen, therefore, that there are many penalties and deprivations visited upon one-parent families. The penalties are somewhat differentiated by the sex of the parent, and it would be foolish to dogmatize on which sex has the harder time of it, although lone mothers very possibly do so, and certainly constitute the majority of lone parents. A comparison of health experience (Chester, 1971; George and Wilding, 1972) suggests that women suffer more stress. They experience a good deal of poor health, with an emphasis on symptoms suggestive of psychosomatic conditions, although it may be that current sex role definitions make it probable that women will more readily translate stress into psychosomatic symptoms or that they will more readily admit to ill-health. The existence of stress and poor health need not be surprising among a group which tends to suffer from economic and social exclusion, stigmatization and normative uncertainty, and over-taxing demands on physical and moral energy. It is likely that break-up of marriage will always bring with it a certain degree of trauma, but much of the difficulty faced by one-parent families is not *entailed* in their situation, and is rather the result of social attitudes, the normal working of social arrangements, and the absence of appropriate social provision. Together these limit access to the various social sources of reward and self-validation and in considerable measure create the "characteristic difficulties" of one-parent families.

It is important to note in all this the significant part played by the general situation of women in society, since many of the problems of lone mothers are particular outcomes of this. Their poverty springs in part from women's lesser training and access to economic opportunity, together with all the assumptions built into labour market practices which tend to unfit women for full economic participation. In consequence of this lone mothers have need to resort to state benefits, where their situation (supplementary benefits rather than insurance payments) reflects the absence of social insurance against broken marriages and the assumption strongly embedded in the system that women are dependents. The lesser social standing and power of female heads of household stem from the generally inferior status of women, and their felt and manifested inability to cope with issues concerning authority derives from the cultural stress on nurturant roles in the upbringing of girls. The anxieties of lone fathers concerning the emotional needs of their children reflect the converse practice and theory of stressing instrumentality in the raising of boys, so that in various contingencies both sexes suffer from the inflexible ascription by sex of conjugal, parental and domestic roles. It may be the case that a single parent cannot adequately cope unaided with servicing a family, but the situation is made worse when incapacities are unnecessarily linked with sex status.

A paradoxical consequence of the situation described above is that the absence of structured provision for the consequences of broken marriage *itself* structures the situation of single parents—by pressing them towards remarriage as the only normatively-sanctioned and institutionally-provided avenue of relief for their manifold (and at least partially socially-induced) problems. Remarriage is undoubtedly the commonest outcome of divorce, and although numbers are difficult to estimate it is probable that at least two-thirds of divorcees remarry. Currently more than a quarter of marriages involve remarriage for one or both of the partners, and this general picture is usually held to demonstrate the continuing popularity of marriage. It could be held, however, that the ethic of conjugality is substantially sustained by the coercive latent consequences of the social processes described here. Lone parents find themselves in a circular situation: because society refuses to endorse or support the one-parent family as a legitimate form, single parents are pressed to remarry; because so many remarry, making single-parenthood a transient status, society is reluctant to support the one-parent family. Certainly in considering the popularity of remarriage we should not ignore the considerably lesser eligibility of available alternatives.

Even in seeking remarriage, however, lone parents face barriers and difficulties. Courtship institutions are age-specific and designed for the young and unencumbered. Courtship skills are probably eroded by age and the experience of marriage, and courtship is anyway difficult under the gaze of children. Women have to cope with problems of sexual reputation and regulation of their sexual activities by social security agencies. Such difficulties are compounded by financial austerity and practical problems of baby-sitting. The basic problem of exposure to eligible partners is difficult for lone parents to solve, even though many of them do manage to solve it. Special clubs, marriage bureaux and personal colunms are used by minorities, but unlike the young and unmarried the majority of lone parents find little social facilitation of their search for potential partners. Our arrangements seem to deprive single parents into wanting to remarry, but to force them to rely on ingenuity and luck to do so.

There are indications in England that the situation for one-parent families in general, and female-headed families in particular, is improving. New forms of income provision are on the political agenda, and a considerable pressure group campaign is developing. More generally, economic prospects and occupational conditions for women are being scrutinized, (as are other opportunities) under the impact of anti-discrimination legislation, and developments here would benefit lone mothers. Social attitudes show signs of changing, and public policy has begun to modify the exclusive preference it has always shown for one particular form of married and family living. Despite such trends, however, there is far to go before the one-parent family could be said to be normalized, accepted and supported as an alternative to domestic orthodoxy. Clearly it would be difficult to argue that the one-parent family should be seen as a preferred form, but this is not required. What is needed is recognition of the facts that a plural society necessarily produces pluralistic forms of the family, and that high levels of instability of marriage are normal in modern society. Coupled with changing thought about the situation of women and a contemporary tendency towards the de-differentiation of conjugal roles, this would lead to the further recognition of how far the many problems associated with one-parent families are the product of institutional and cultural factors which could be modified by appropriate policies. Not all such problems or their sources are policy-responsive, but many of them are, and a very fit topic for discussion and research, therefore, is how some of the inequalities currently suffered by one-parent families might be removed.

References

Central Advisory Council for Education (England) (1967). *Children and their Primary Schools.* Vol. 2, *Research and Surveys.* (The Plowden Report). London: HMSO.

Chester, R. (1971). Health and marriage breakdown: experience of a sample of divorced women. *British Journal of Preventive and Social Medicine,* **25,** 231–235.

Chester, R. and Streather, J. (1972). The stigma of divorce. *Social Service News,* **2,** 12–15.

Cockburn, C. and Heclo, H. (1974). Income maintenance for one-parent families in other countries. Appendix 3 of the *Report of the Committee on One-Parent Families.* London: HMSO.

Committee on One-Parent Families (1974). *Report* (2 volumes). (The Finer Report). London: HMSO.

Ferri, E. (1973). Characteristics of motherless families. *British Journal of Social Work,* **3,** 91–100.

Garvey, A. (1974). Women in pubs. *New Society,* 21 February.

George, V. and Wilding, P. (1972). *Motherless Families.* London: Routledge and Kegan Paul.

Goode, W. J. (1965). *Women in Divorce.* New York: The Free Press.

Hart, N. (1976). *When Marriage Ends.* London: Tavistock Publications.

Hunt, A. (1973). *Families and their Needs.* (2 volumes). London: HMSO.

Marsden, D. (1973). *Mothers Alone.* Harmondsworth, Middx.: Penguin Books.

Morgan, D. H. J. (1975). *Social Theory and the Family.* London: Routledge and Kegan Paul.

Rowntree, G. (1955). Early childhood in broken families. *Population Studies,* **8,** 247–263.

Susser, M. and Watson, W. (1971). *Sociology in Medicine.* Oxford: Oxford University Press.

Turner, C. (1969). *Family and Kinship in Modern Britain.* London: Routledge and Kegan Paul.

Inequalities in Large Families: More of the Same or Different?

HILARY LAND

Department of Social Administration, University of Bristol, Bristol, England

The number of large families in Britain has been declining in the last ten years. A study of recent demographic trends concluded:

> the third and subsequent child is certainly becoming an increasing rarity. In 1965 such children still formed 31 per cent of all births, and by 1974 the proportions was down to 20 per cent so really large families are becoming very rare indeed. 15,700 children were born in 1961 to women who had had five previous children; by 1973 the figure was down to about 5,000 and the 1975 figure may be as low as 3,000 (Eversley, 1976, 33).

In the future then, if these trends continue, only a very small minority of children may experience being brought up in a large family. Nevertheless there are still a substantial number of children who are currently members of a large family. For example, the National Child Development Study, a cohort study of over 17,000 children born in one week in 1958 contained 18 per cent or one in six children living in families with five or more children, (Wedge and Prosser, 1973, 11). These children have only just reached adulthood.

The fact that large families are more likely to be poor than small families has been just as evident in post-war Britain as in earlier decades. For example, the study *Circumstances of Families*, conducted ten years ago by the Ministry of Social Security (now the Department of Health and Social Security) showed that families with five children were three times as likely as two-child families to have an income below the supplementary benefit level current at the time. (The level of income paid according to the scales paid by the Supplementary Benefits Commission is often taken as an "official" minimum income.)

For larger families, the probability of experiencing poverty was higher still and the same study showed that large families were more likely to be living in overcrowded accommodation. Nearly a third of those with four children and nearly two-thirds of those with six or more children were overcrowded, compared with one in ten of all families. *The General Household Survey*, carried out more recently in 1971 (Office of Population Censuses and Surveys, 1973a) revealed a similar pattern and in addition, the proportions living in defective housing increased with family size. The evidence also shows that fathers of large families work on average longer hours and the mother's earnings are more likely to be a crucial factor in keeping the family out of poverty, although the proportion of mothers in paid employment decreases with family size. For obvious reasons a woman's earnings are likely to be intermittent if she has several children to care for but, more surprisingly, so too are the earnings of the man with a large family. In 1966, men with large families were twice as likely as those with small families to experience sickness or unemployment (Ministry of Social Security, 1966, 44). There are indications now that rising unemployment hits men with several children disproportionately hard. In 1971, the unemployment rate of all family heads with five children was three times the average male unemployment rate and for the unskilled man with five children the rate was six times greater (Office of Population Censuses and Surveys, 1973b). Thus the incomes of large families are not only likely to be low but also precarious.

We do not know why fathers of large families are more prone to sickness or unemployment. Is it because at any point in time a sample of such men is likely to contain a higher proportion of older men than a sample of men with only one or two children? Or are men who have large families less educated and less skilled, or are men with the largest families concentrated in geographical areas with higher than average unemployment? Is their poorer health a reflection of substandard housing, or inadequate diet currently experienced, or a result of childhood deprivation? Whatever the reasons, substantial inequalities between large and small families still exist.

In this paper I shall not continue to explore and compare the extent of inequalities between families of different sizes but rather concentrate on inequalities *within* families. In other words I shall concentrate on those inequalities in large families which I take to be more of the same as, rather than different from, those experienced by smaller families. I shall argue that by looking at the impact of poverty in its various dimensions among one of the groups where it shows up most starkly, namely large families, we can understand much more about the causes and results of inequalities within the family both between the generations and between the sexes. Who bears the brunt of a low income, poor and overcrowded housing, an inadequate diet and so on? Is poverty born evenly by all members of the family or not? The answers to these questions are important because they might help to explain, for example, why some individuals in a family escape from poverty while others do not. Why do some children of a family in their adult life perpetuate the disadvantages experienced by their parents? For example, in my own study of large families (Land, 1969) nearly half of the parents I interviewed came from large families themselves. This appears to support the cycle of deprivation thesis that large families, especially poor large families, in turn breed more poor, large families. However, the parents I interviewed were *different* from their siblings, the majority of whom had had small families. Clearly part of the explanation may be found in individual differences, but I wish to explore some of the social and economic factors which affect the pattern of distribution of resources within the family thus putting some individuals within the family at an advantage over others.

In many studies of standards of living the family or household is taken as the basic unit of analysis and there is an assumption, usually remaining implicit, that financial resources going into the family, irrespective of their source and to whom they are first paid, are very largely pooled and shared out among members of the family according to some collective notion of their needs. Economists talk of "joint" family or household utilities but pay very little attention to the means by which the members of the family unit arrive at a definition of their collective needs or how the responsibility for providing for those needs should be met by its different members. This is not to say that there are no beliefs or views about how these needs and responsibilities *ought* to be met, but the factors which determine such beliefs and the extent to which they structure the actual behaviour of individuals inside and outside the family have been taken for granted and rarely examined.

The Division of Financial Responsibility: Housekeeping

How are responsibilities for purchasing and paying for food, fuel, housing costs, clothing, etc., divided between husband and wife? Where does the money come from to make these payments: what proportion of the husband's earnings and how much of the wife's earnings contribute to collective household items and how much is kept back for personal expenditure? How do these proportions change as family size increases and earnings vary? And what contribution do earning children still living at home, make to the collective purse?

Much of the historical evidence on patterns of housekeeping came from surveys of living standards, many of which have been particularly concerned with measuring poverty. Poor families' spending patterns have been rather more thoroughly investigated than those of middle and higher income families. This has meant that there has been a tendency to overlook contributions which husbands make to collective items of expenditure, in addition to the housekeeping allowance given to the wife. Because poor families have little choice but to buy most things "little and often" and because one general finding which seems to apply to all income groups, is that wives are more likely to be responsible for making frequent (daily or weekly) purchases, and husbands for less frequent (monthly or quarterly) payments, there has been a tendency to assume that "the housekeeping allowance" allotted to the wife has to meet all items of household expenditure. Therefore, any part of his earnings which the husband keeps back or is returned to him by his wife, is for his own personal expenditure (and in the view of those who moralize about the poor, spent entirely on drink and tobacco).

This simple division of financial resources still applies to many low income families and it was, and is still, true that the amount of money handled by the wife is a good indication of that family's (in particular the wife's and children's) standard of living. As a social commentator, Eden, wrote nearly two centuries ago:

> There is perhaps, no better mode of ascertaining what degree of comfort is enjoyed by a labourer's family, than by learning what portion of his weekly earnings he commits to his wife's disposal. It makes very material difference whether he or she holds the purse strings. That he can earn the most, is granted, but she can make those earnings go the farthest . . . (Eden, 1797, 625).

Much more recently, Michael Young on the basis of evidence gleaned from surveys on family expenditure and patterns of saving, and on standards of nutrition and poverty, also concluded that:

> the husband-wife contract is of key importance to the family standard of living (Young, 1952, 305).

He also emphasized that it could not be assumed that all members of the family shared the same standard of living, particularly as family circumstances changed:

> The financial burden of having an extra child was not . . . shared equally by all members of the family, but fell with especial severity upon the mother and upon previous children (Young, 1952, 312).

Another study conducted in Aberdeen in the fifties, finding also that housekeeping allowances were not very responsive to changing family size, concluded that:

> the relatively unchanging level of housekeeping resources in a wage-earning household helped to perpetuate the husband's dominant position in financial matters, and, as the family grew, placed an increasing premium on the wife's managing ability and her capacity to sacrifice her own needs to those of others. However efficient she might be, it seemed probable that standards of living would have to be lowered as successive children were born, each adding his claim to a share of the limited house-keeping resources (Rowntree, 1954, 213–214).

Part of this was due to the fact that the husband's gross earnings had not necessarily risen with the growth of the family, although his net earnings were increased by the operation of the tax system. However, it was clear from this study that the husband's personal expenditure was decreased proportionately less than the wife's *per capita* housekeeping allowance, and this mattered because then, as now, she was almost invariably responsible for buying the food (see Table I). Husbands whose incomes had increased, spent more on domestic items or saved more, but not necessarily at the expense of their outlay on personal miscellaneous and recreational items.

TABLE I

Division of responsibility for household items of expenditure (1971)

Who usually dealt with	Buying food	Pay for gas, electricity	Pay for rent/rates	Pay for mortgage	Dealing with any surplus
	%	%	%	%	%
Wife	89	49	61	30	36
Husband	3	38	29	59	20
Both or either	7	10	6	11	43
Other answer	1	3	4	—	1
	100 = 1877	100 = 1877	100 = 896 (tenants)	100 = 978 (owner occupiers)	100 = 1877

Source: Todd and Jones (1972).

More recent evidence demonstrates how the housekeeping allowance given to the wife by the husband may lag behind rising prices. In 1975, both the National Consumer Council and *Woman's Own* carried out studies of housekeeping money. Both studies found that in the previous 12 months more than one in four of husbands had not increased their housekeeping allowances at all and among the lowest paid (husbands earning less than £20 per week) half of the wives had received no increase. Altogether, among the 4,000 readers who returned their questionnaire, *Woman's Own* found that one in five mothers had received no increase and among those with more children the proportion was higher: nearly a third of mothers with three or more children were having to manage on the same money as twelve months earlier. On average, men had passed on less than half their pay rises to their wives and this meant for many that in real terms their housekeeping allowance had diminished. Michael Young found a similar pattern in two smaller studies conducted in Bethnal Green and Camden Town (Syson and Young, 1975).

It cannot be assumed that the only contribution which husbands make to the financial upkeep of the home is in the form of a housekeeping allowance. Many households have very flexible, joint arrangements. An interesting small study of housekeeping patterns among manual workers was recently conducted in Edinburgh by Ann Gray (Gray, 1974) and she distinguished between two major types of arrangements. In the first the husband keeps or is given back his own personal spending money and he pays for one or more major items consumed collectively by the household. The second involves the wife being given an allowance but the husband pays for two or more collective items himself. She found the first arrangement less flexible than the second. She examined the cultural backgrounds of the families and other characteristics of their marital relationships. Those who had clearly demarcated financial responsibilities also shared household and childcare rather less, they had few friends in common and spent more of their leisure time in separate activities. A much larger proportion of these couples came from homes in which the father had been in a traditional primary sector occupation—mining, crofting, fishing or farming. Where men have unskilled, fatiguing jobs there is a greater likelihood that a fixed allowance will be given. Older or less fit men behave similarly because they want to keep the option of whether or not to work overtime: they do not wish to accustom their wives to a standard of living they might not be willing or able to maintain.

In households in which there is a rigid housekeeping system the wives are more likely to take paid employment. This is so that they can increase the amount of money over which they have some control as well as having additional resources for the family. As Table II shows, the lower the occupational status of the father, the greater the proportion of the wife's earnings spent on general housekeeping. However, it is clear from Table III, that in many families the wife's earnings make an important contribution to general household expenditure. The amount of money coming directly to the wife whether through her own earnings, the housekeeping allowance or family allowances (the only state benefit paid directly to her rather than to her husband) has a very important bearing on the standard of living of all members of the family.

TABLE II
Allocation of wife's earnings by occupation of husband

Occupation of husband	Per cent of wife's earnings spent on general housekeeping
Unskilled manual	69
Semi-skilled manual	64
Skilled manual	55
Managerial/Professional	50

Source: Todd and Jones (1972).

TABLE III
The contribution wives' earnings make to the family budget

Items on which most of earnings were spent	Per cent of married women in paid employment reporting these items as accounting for most of their earnings
General housekeeping	56
Clothes for self	26
Clothes for children	26
Holidays	18
Household appliances	21
Personal Expenditure	5

Source: Hunt (1968).

What difference do earning children make to the household finances? Working children's contributions to housekeeping are unresponsive to changing economic circumstances. The amount given to mothers for board and lodging seems to be fixed as much by custom as by reference to the actual cost of the child's keep. In 1965 I found that earning children in the large families I studied in London gave their parents about £3 a week. There seemed to be little variation. Millward who, a year or so later, also found a customary amount of £3 to £4 in Manchester, concluded that:

what determines these amounts is still to be investigated, but the pressures of custom and tradition do seem to be important within the more closely-knit communities studied. (Millward, 1968).

More recently in 1975, the National Consumer Council's study of 1,830 families showed that young earners living at home had given their mothers only an extra £1 although their weekly earnings had increased on average by £3·45 in the previous year. This meant that out of an average weekly income of £27 they were only contributing £6·68 to the housekeeping money. It is therefore dangerous to conclude that earning children living at home necessarily increases the *whole family's* standard of living.

The Division of Resources within the Family

FOOD

Expenditure on food is likely to fall if housekeeping money is unresponsive to changing prices and low income, large families are more likely than small families to be in this situation. This does not necessarily mean nutritional standards fall, but if staple items like milk, bread, meat, eggs, potatoes increase rapidly in price there is no guarantee that the cheaper foods available and chosen will be as nutritious. When I did my study ten years ago these items were much cheaper and there was considerable reliance on bread and potatoes among the poorer families. Two families, one with ten children, the other with fourteen ate 100 pounds of potatoes and 20 large loaves of bread a week. These are extreme examples, but how would such families economize today? Dependence on school and welfare milk was high, accounting for one-third of the total milk consumption for one-quarter of the families interviewed. Ten years ago these were provided free to all children, now they are subject to a means test and we know that the uptake of these benefits is low where the father is in full-time employment.

If nutritional standards do fall, and we cannot be at all confident that they have not done so amongst low income families especially large families, who in the family is most vulnerable? In my study of large families it was very evident that the mother was the most likely to go without food for she was the most dependent on meals provided at home. Over half of them had no cooked meal in the middle of the day. That in itself does not necessarily mean they were undernourished but a quarter had no breakfast and nothing more than a sandwich for lunch. One in twelve *never* had a cooked meal. It was clear that the father's needs were put first, then the children's and finally the mother's. Averaging out food consumption per head in a family is therefore a misleading practice.

This is not a new phenomenon. Over fifty years ago Seebohm

Rowntree, one of the pioneers in the study and measurement of standards of living made a similar point. For example, on the basis of a study he conducted just before the First World War among agricultural workers he wrote:

> The women and children suffer from underfeeding to a much greater extent than men. It is tacitly agreed that the man must have a certain minimum of food in order that he may be able to perform the muscular work demanded of him; and the provision of this minimum, in the case of families with small incomes involves a degree of underfeeding for the women and children greater than is shown by the average figures we present (Rowntree, 1913).

Rowntree noticed that the remark "for the man only" was often written by the side of the menus he had collected from these families. Indeed a saying common in one of the areas he studied was:

> the women and children look at the meat and eat the potatoes.

In the 1930s studies of the health and nutritional status of women showed a similar pattern (Spring-Rice, 1939) and when married women joined the labour market in large numbers during the Second World War the extent of malnutrition among women was revealed.

CLOTHING

The evidence we have on expenditure on clothing also suggests that some members of the family are more likely to go without new clothing than others. In the large families study it was the mother once again who was the most likely to go without. One in eight of the mothers I interviewed had not had a new coat, for example, since their marriage and they had all been married at least ten years. Outdoor shoes were also a problem. While second-hand clothing may be just as effective as new clothing in keeping the wearer warm, it should not be forgotten that clothing affects a person's appearance and with it their sense of self-respect or their morale. The question about the mother's clothing was the most sensitive question on my questionnaire; more sensitive than questions about the family income or knowledge and use of birth control methods. Several mothers I interviewed said they felt ashamed to visit their children's school, for example, because they believed other parents and the teachers who were better dressed would look down on them. While parent-teacher contacts are determined by many factors if it is believed that such contacts are a good thing, then anything which diminishes the confidence of parents to visit schools should be a cause of concern.

HOUSING

Who bears the brunt of sub-standard accommodation and overcrowding? Sleeping arrangements are obviously affected by overcrowding. Children sharing bedrooms may or may not disturb each other's sleep, children sharing beds almost certainly will. Lack of sleep may affect physcial growth as much as poor nutrition and a tired child will not attend so well to the teacher at school. The National Child Development study found that over half the disadvantaged children in their study (i.e. children from a one-parent family or large family, who were badly housed and from a low-income family) shared a bed, compared with less than one in ten of ordinary children. One in twenty-two of these children, ten times as many as ordinary children, wet the bed they were sharing (Wedge and Prosser, 1973, 26). In my study of large families nearly one in six children were sharing a bed. Younger children were more likely to share than older children. Parents who share bedrooms or even beds with their children may also have disturbed sleep. Whose need for undisturbed rest is given priority in the family and at whose expense is it obtained? Father may be allowed to sleep in front of the television all evening; mother is much less likely to be able to do so. In addition, she is more likely to have to get up in the night to see to the crying baby for although men are beginning to take a share in the tasks involved in caring for children, there is a very long way to go before they are shared equally between parents. As with food, there is a widespread view that the needs of the person with a full day's *paid* work in front of them are more important than those of the full-time housewife, and one can see that this view prevails because domestic work is taken for granted and so remains invisible. However, the tired mother will not be as efficient a manager and will be less patient with, or attentive to, her children.

Individuals also need privacy. Children need peace and quiet to do homework for example. Older members of the family may wish to entertain friends without involving all the younger members. Whose interests get sacrificed for whom? One mother I interviewed was faced with the dilemma of allowing her eldest son who had just started work, to move out of the bedroom he shared with a couple of younger brothers into the sitting room which was the only room in the house in which a member of the family could entertain with any degree of privacy. The younger boys were always interfering with his belongings and he was threatening to leave home if he could not have a room of his own.

The ability to pay for fuel will also affect the use of space in a house and again those members of the family who are at home for most of the day may be more affected by necessary economies on fuel than those who come home in the evening when it is "worth" having a fire on.

TIME

Time is a resource which may also be scarce (indeed in one sense it is the only scarce resource) and there is a limit to how much time money can buy. The richer parents in the sample of large families I interviewed complained about lack of time. The mothers regretted that they could not spend as much time as they would like with each child and those who had very young children felt that their needs were so immediate that they would give their attention to them while the father gave his attention to the older children. This lack of individual attention which means, for example, that children in large families are read and talked to less by adults than children in small families, may partly explain why the verbal achievement of children of large families in *all* income groups is lower than for children from small families. Numerical ability is not correlated with family size.

Mothers in families with sufficient income could afford to buy the time of others. Housework was therefore less of a burden. Among the majority of large families in my sample, housework was the responsibility of the mother, with children and fathers helping sometimes. Other studies have shown that mothers in paid employment do not necessarily receive more help in the house either from their husbands or their children than women who are full-time housewives (Hunt, 1968). Also although girls do rather more than boys, children help comparatively little in the home (Barker, 1972). In times of family crisis, such as illness of the mother, girls are more likely than boys to be kept home from school to help in the house. The National Child Development Study found that twelve per cent of 16-year-olds had been kept home from school to help at home in the twelve months prior to the survey interview (Fogelman, 1976). The preliminary analyses did not distinguish between boys and girls but it is highly probable that the percentage of girls would be considerably higher than for boys. The difference is partly accounted for by the belief that girls are more useful at home and partly because a girl's education at school is accorded less importance by parents than a boys. This is an example of how a social service is used differentially by individual members of the family.

Conclusions

The standard of living of individual members of the family may differ quite markedly and it cannot be assumed that all earning members pool their wages for the purchase of goods and services for the family as a whole. In a period of inflation or during periods when the family is growing in size the amount of money controlled by the wife is a critical determinant of the standard of living of herself and dependent children. Extra money earned by older children or the husband may or may not be channelled into the family purse. Housekeeping allowances in what is often taken to be the more traditional working-class family where there is a rigid segregation of responsibilities and activities between husband and wife may respond only slowly to changing circumstances and needs. If the wife has paid employment she may be able to cushion the general housekeeping fund from the effects of inflation to some extent. If not, she is entirely dependent on her husband's willingness and ability to increase her housekeeping money, and on the only form of social security benefits paid directly to her, namely family allowances. Most social security benefits are still based on the assumption that the family needs can be met by paying benefits directly to the man and that it is only the loss of his income which needs replacing at times of sickness or unemployment.

We have looked at patterns of inequality which have roots going far back into the past. They are patterns which had some justification when the maintenance of a man's physical strength was essential in order to keep a job. However, we should ask whether social policies perpetuate or compensate for these inequalities. In the past some policies clearly made the situation worse. For example, some public assistance committees in the 1930s gave a lower allowance to mothers who were breast-feeding their babies on the grounds that they would need to buy less milk! (Hannington, 1937). Today the provision of meals and milk for schoolchildren helps to improve the nutritional status of children but there are no special provisions for parents. The father's needs will be given priority within the family anyway and he may benefit from subsidized meals at work, but what about mothers—the member of the family most likely to be dependent on meals at home? A woman who is tired because she is undernourished is less likely to provide a high standard of care for her family.

Similarly, if the family is receiving supplementary benefits then it may be possible for all members to get a clothing grant, but in poor families with the father in full-time employment, only the children may get help with school clothing. Fathers may get clothing or uniform provided by employers but there are no additional sources of clothing for the wife of a low-wage earner who is a full-time wife and mother.

The impact of a low income, bad housing, and insufficient food, is not borne equally by all members of the family. Resources are allocated by reference to custom or tradition and the interests of some members of the family are sacrificed to the interests of others. In particular, it is noticeable that in many respects the mother of the family puts the needs of her husband and her children before her own. Many of our social policies which in practice are directed at individual members of the family rather than the family as a whole, often reinforce, rather than compensate for, these inequalities between members of the family. Should we be content with this, particularly if we are concerned to reduce inequalities between men and women or boys and girls? But if we are not, is it realistic to think social policies could achieve a different distribution of resources between members of a family? For example, the General Household Survey (1971), using as an indicator of seriousness of illness, whether or not a doctor was consulted, found that:

> very young children were the most likely subjects of consultation about chronic sickness, particularly boys of whom nearly three out of four were taken to or visited by a doctor, or had a parent discuss their condition with a doctor by telephone, at least once during the period of their restriction. This suggests that small boys not only are more liable to acute sickness than small girls, but also that *the nature of their sickness is more serious or more seriously regarded.* (My italics) (Office of Population Censuses and Surveys, 1973, 299).

In other words, customs *may* also determine who uses a social service which in theory is available to every member of a family. However, until we examine and understand why and how resources are used by and allocated between different members of families unequally, it is difficult to answer these questions. It is clear, however, that many social policies do not always compensate for these inequalities.

References

Barker, D. (1972). Young people and their homes: spoiling and 'keeping close' in a South Wales Town. *Sociological Review*, **20**, 569–590.

Eden, F. M. (1797). *State of the Poor.* Vol. 1.

Eversley, D. (1976). Demographic change and the demand for housing. In *The Uncertain Future*. Edited by M. Buxton and E. Craven. London: Centre for Studies in Social Policy.

Fogelman, K. (1976). *Britain's Sixteen-Year-Olds*. London: National Children's Bureau.

Gray, A. (1974). *The Working-Class Family as an Economic Unit*. Ph.D. Thesis (unpublished). Edinburgh University.

Hannington, W. (1937). *The Problem of the Distressed Areas*. London: Victor Gollancz.

Hunt, A. (1968). *A Survey of Women's Employment*. Vol. II. London: HMSO.

Land, H. (1969). *Large Families in London*. London: Bell and Sons.

Millward, N. (1968). Family status and behaviour at work. *Sociological Review*, **16**, 149–164.

Ministry of Social Security (1966). *Circumstances of Families*. London: HMSO.

Office of Population Censuses and Surveys (1973a). *Census 1971, Great Britain.* London: HMSO.

Office of Population Censuses and Surveys (1973b). *The General Household Survey: Introductory Report.* London: HMSO.

Rowntree, G. (1954). The finances of founding a family. *Scottish Journal of Political Economy,* **1** (3).

Rowntree, S. (1913). *How the Labourer Lives.* London: Nelson.

Spring-Rice, M. (1939). *Working-Class Wives.* Harmondsworth, Middx.: Penguin Books.

Syson, L. and Young, M. (1975). Poverty in Bethnal Green. In *Poverty Report* (1974). Edited by M. Young. London: Temple Smith.

Todd, J. E. and Jones, L. N. (1972). *Matrimonial Property.* London: HMSO.

Wedge, P. and Prosser, H. (1973). *Born to Fail.* London: Arrow Books.

Woman's Own. (1975). Housekeeping survey. 20th September.

Young, M. (1952). Distribution of income within the family. *British Journal of Sociology,* **3,** 305–321.

Alternatives to the Family

D. H. J. MORGAN

Department of Sociology
University of Manchester, Manchester, England

Introduction

Discussions of alternatives to the family often appear to follow the same pattern and to suffer the same fate as discussions between academics about alternatives to the conventional examination system. The traditional three-hour unseen paper is found to be defective in several important respects and possible alternatives such as term papers, continuous assessment, multiple-choice papers and so on are examined. One by one each alternative is found to raise severe pedagogic or practical difficulties and the traditional system, perhaps with some minor modifications, remains in the face of the collapse of an exhausted opposition. Some more courageous bodies may, however, propose and set in motion mixed systems of assessment.

Similarly, discussions of alternatives to the family tend to conclude that, although there may be some increasing experimentation on the fringes, the conjugally-based, nuclear family is here to stay as the majority option. Thus it is likely that most sociologists would agree with the following statement:

> The future will bring not any one pattern, but a *greater differentiation of patterns*. The decision between solutions will become increasingly an individual, not a social, matter . . . There will probably be a majority or normal solution, with greater tolerance for minority solutions, so that each particular family shall have a more genuine range of choice (Folsom, 1934).

It is perhaps salutary to note that this particular projection was made over forty years ago. Similarly Goode, writing in 1971, notes that:

> In the United States almost all alternative family structures exist within and indeed depend upon, a surrounding social structure in which older family patterns are maintained (Goode, 1971).

He goes on to conclude that:

> Our social structure continues to make the husband-wife-child household the most convenient; and besides, most people are socialized to accept it, even if grudgingly.

More enthusiastically, another contemporary author asserts:

> . . . the nuclear family will not only persist into the twenty-first century but it will be stronger than ever (Yorburg, 1973, p. 191).

She repeats the argument for greater tolerance of minority forms.

In this paper I shall not follow the well-trodden path of considering the fate of "free-love" in the Soviet Union (Geiger, 1968; Bronfenbrenner, 1968) or the process whereby familism came to be re-asserted within Israeli kibbutzim (Talmon, 1962). Nor shall I say a great deal about the more recent analyses of continuing strength of the family in China (Davin, 1976) or the problems facing modern intentional communities, or communes in Britain and the United States (Abrams and McCulloch, 1976; Kanter, 1973; Rigby, 1974). The object of this paper is slightly different, perhaps more narrow: it is to consider what is entailed in the phrase "alternatives to the family" and some of the ways in which this problem might be re-formulated.

In the first place, of course, the phrase implies that there is something wrong with the contemporary family and that, consequently, the search for alternatives is to be desired. Criticisms, or implied criticisms of the family have come from a variety of sources in recent years. Writers with a radical psycho-analytical interest, such as Henry, Laing and especially Cooper, have extended accounts of the families of persons labelled as schizophrenics to a more general indictment of the modern family with its patterns of mystification and scapegoating, its spirals of misunderstandings, its potential for terror and violence (Henry, 1972; Laing, 1971; Cooper, 1972).

Members of the contemporary feminist movement, particularly those working within a Marxist tradition, have analysed the dual role of the family in maintaining the subordination and exploitation of women, chiefly through the institution of housework, and of reproducing, socially as well as biologically, the capitalist system over the generations (Barker and Allen, 1976; Gardiner, 1975; Oakley, 1974).

More specifically sociological critiques of the family have been relatively rare, one of the more original and persuasive being that provided by Sennett who argues that the intensification of family life in contemporary society freezes individuals and ultimately whole communities into adolescent modes of relating to the world, fearful of opening up to the complexity and diversity of modern urban life

(Sennett, 1971). This argument is captured in the title of one of his books, *Families Against the City* (1970) and the theme of the narrowness and enclosed intimacy of privatized family living has been a growing one in some recent sociological writings (Skolnick, 1973). Elsewhere, the growing concern over domestic violence, while not usually leading to a search for alternatives, has sharpened our awareness of some of the defects of the isolated nuclear family (Borland, 1976) and the prolifera-tion of collections of readings or symposia with such titles as *The Nuclear Family in Crisis* (Gordon, 1972) or *The Family in Search of a Future* (Otto, 1970) bear witness to all the concerns we have mentioned so far. Yet it is possible to exaggerate the extent of these critiques and it is likely that the Archbishop of Canterbury's recent calls for a strengthening of family life have been at least as influential as, and certainly more widely publicized than, all these indictments and critiques. We may also note the reported findings of a survey that found that, out of a sample of nearly 15,000 sixteen-year-olds, only 3 per cent were opposed to marriage altogether (Sandilands, 1976).

Critics and supporters of the family alike tend to share at least one assumption in common, namely a relatively uncritical use of the term "family". The assumption is that there is a partially fixed and clearly defined entity called "the family" which can be said to be performing recognizable functions or dysfunctions for the individuals who compose it and for the society of which it is a part. The very notion of "alter-natives to the family" implies a search for something which is both family and not-family, something which carries over some features of these postulated family functions into new patterns of living.

Definitions of the family normally revolve around three interconnected elements: marriage, parenthood and common residence. Yet each one of these three elements poses further problems of definition. Few of us, I suspect, would be willing to restrict our definition of marriage to those unions blessed by the church or recognized by the state; some recogni-tion would be given to "common-law" marriages or to couples living together "as if" they were married. We would certainly wish to give some recognition to the growing proportion of the remarried in the population and to patterns of "serial monogamy". More debate might surround homosexual partnerships or patterns of group or complex marriage. Similarly, extended discussions could revolve around the nature of parenthood. These might include, among other topics, the significance of the difference between biologically and socially defined parenthood: the extent to which the idea of parenthood depends upon some notion of marriage, given the importance of the mother-child, single-parent family in many parts of the world (Adams, 1960); and the role of godparents or ritual co-parents in countries where such relationships continue to be defined and to perform important functions (Mintz and Wolf, 1950). Finally, the concept of "common residence" would appear to be a more simple matter until it is realized that the census finds it necessary to provide several paragraphs explaining its definition of "household" (Stacey, 1969) and that arguments over what precisely constitutes co-habitation sometimes have consequences that are far from academic.

If it were possible to agree about the definitions of the three constituents of a definition of "family" we are still faced with difficulties over how these constituents might be combined. We may agree that a situation where all three elements, marriage, parenthood and common residence, are present is one which is closest to most people's image or ideal model of the family. Yet it can also be argued that where any two or even any one of these elements are present we have a situation which has at least some "family like" qualities. Thus couples may undertake a commitment to live together without benefit of state or clergy and one-parent families (LeMasters, 1970) or childless couples (Veevers, 1973) may be a chosen or preferred state for at least some members of these categories. Thus our notion of "the family" contains many forms of living within it and the dividing line between family and non-family, or between the family and any possible alternative, may consequently be much more difficult to draw. Also we have only considered so far some of the more formal elements of a definition and that while this discussion is not merely academic but reflects actual ways of living and experiencing family and family-type relationships it does not begin to touch upon some more profound sources of variation such as in the sexual division of labour or relationships with kin.

I would suggest, therefore, that a discussion of "alternatives to the family" in terms of alternative *forms* or *structures*, as if we could place the family in one column and various alternatives in another completely discrete column, is of limited value. (In passing it may be noted that the use of the term "commune" as a proposed alternative to the family poses at least as many problems as the use of the term "family".) Rather I should like to suggest here two rather different ways of looking at the problem which may, in various ways, cut across distinctions between family and non-family. The first is an approach which looks at different social *networks* and the second is in terms of alternative *processes*. I do not claim any particular originality here, but I suggest that these orientations may be more fruitful in opening up the discussion than stark contrasts between families and communes or some of the more simple calls to "smash monogamy" or "abolish the family".

Social Networks

The idea of a social network has had a relatively short but highly fruitful history in sociology and social anthropology (Bott, 1971; Mitchell, 1969). In essence, the concept points to the simple fact that any one individual (or couple, or family) is linked to a variety of other individuals. What "linked to" actually means needs to be specified but it may include everything from simple knowledge of, or recognition of, the others to more tangible exchanges of advice, gossip, goods or services. Some of these individuals in a particular network will be known to the others; where many individuals in a personal network are known to each other in this way we speak of a close-knit network and where few are known to each other, we speak of a loose-knit network. In this latter instance, an individual will know and be known to several others but these others will not, as a rule, be known to each other. The concept of a social network has been found to be particularly fruitful in analyzing relationships in urban environments, characterized by considerable change and mobility.

Clearly there are many refinements that can and should be made to this simple concept, presented here in its baldest form, but the idea is of particular relevance when considering alternatives to the family. Urban communes, for example, may be described as close-knit but relatively open (i.e. unbounded) networks unlike religious communities, such as the Shakers or the Hutterites, which may be characterized as close-knit but closed networks. Analysed in terms of social networks, urban communes may, in some cases be seen to have more in common with other networks of families or individuals who have interests or occupations in common or who associate together for some particular purpose such as coping with some mental or physical disability in a family or to achieve some local political or social goal. Networks may be networks of kin but they may also consist of friends, neighbours, colleagues or workmates. Different categories of relationships within a network may be selected or mobilized for particular purposes; thus kin may be chosen in times of sickness or pregnancy while friends may be chosen for advice on emotional problems (Litwak and Szelenyi, 1969). The point about network analysis is that no prior or assumed significance need be given to family or kinship ties (using these terms in the conventional sense to refer to relationships established through blood or marriage) as against other kinds of relationships; the network as a whole is considered and the relative or different significance of its parts should emerge through closer analysis.

Literature may provide us with several examples of social networks in action. Thus Dickens' *Our Mutual Friend* (the very title conveys a theme

of network analysis) is a brilliant example of a gradually unfolding network and this theme of the changing network over time is elaborated in
fascinating detail in Anthony Powell's sequence of novels, *A Dance to the
Music of Time*. In real life, the much-examined Bloomsbury group
provides us with an example of a changing and effective network. Here
we had an elite of friends based partly upon kinship, but more upon
common intellectual (in this case, Cambridge) antecedents, common or
close residence and evolving common interests and identities. Some of
the members of this network, indeed, expressed a marked distaste for
family relationships and obligations and elaborated, in their place, what
might be described as an ideology of friendship. What was particularly
interesting about the group was the extent to which, in many instances,
conventional classifications of distinctions between marital relationships, sexual relationships and friendships were explicitly obscured or
minimized. The very fuzziness of the "Bloomsbury" group, the ambiguity about who was "in" or "out" and by what criteria this was to be
decided, is a reflection of the nature of most urban social networks as
opposed to clearly bounded and defined groups.

It is easy to see the practical importance of social networks. They may
provide channels through which news and assistance may be mobilized
in the case of some personal trouble; in the Bloomsbury case, for
example, it would be possible to analyse the way in which human
resources were mobilized at the times of Virginia Woolf's breakdowns
or suicide attempt. Indeed, looking at relationships in terms of networks
should encourage us to examine events and processes rather than static
structures. For children or adolescents, relatively open social networks
may provide a source of surrogate parents, adult companions or confi-
dants who are less involved in the immediate tensions of day-to-day
family living. Slightly more formally, Stoller has described how his
concept of an "intimate network of families" arose out of a family
workshop (Stoller, 1970) while the family therapist, Speck and his
associates have elaborated and described the uses of "network therapy"
(Speck and Attneave, 1974). Just as earlier therapists turned their
attentions from the individual to the total family situation, so these
therapists turn from the relatively isolated family to the network of
relationships in which it is placed.

While it would be possible to extend this discussion of the positive use
of social networks and perhaps to make suggestions as to how such networks might be encouraged or strengthened, perhaps the more immediate importance of this approach is in its potential for changing the
ways in which we see the family. Networks do not represent new
discoveries or new kinds of relationships; rather they represent new

ways of looking at already existing relationships. While there are, no doubt, some important differences between familial and non-familial relationships, it is likely that these differences are often over-stressed in our culture. Analysis in terms of social networks enables us to concentrate on what familial relationships may have in common with other primary-type relationships and to examine some of the effective ways in which family members are linked to the wider community.

Social Processes

One mistaken way of looking at social networks and one which may sometimes be encouraged by some of the more formal diagrammatic representations of such networks in the literature would be in terms of relatively static alternative *structures*. Networks, like the family itself, represent social *processes*; members die, move away, become involved in other networks while others move in. More generally, we should begin to look at the question of the family and its alternatives in terms of different kinds of processes which, like the concept of social networks, may sometimes cut across clear distinctions between family and non-family. One kind of process, particularly associated with the family and generally understood in both biological and social terms, appears to place individuals in a sequence of events which are defined as natural or inevitable (Ineichen, 1977). Thus marriage is seen as being identified with the attainment of full adult status or, in more popular terms, with "settling down" while the single status may be regarded as less "natural", as a problem demanding sympathy and a solution or as a source of other problems: ("What she needs is a man"; "what he needs is a wife to look after him"). Once married, couples are expected to have children and childlessness is, again, regarded as a situation for personal or moral concern. Similarly, families with one child are urged, at least indirectly, to "complete their families" with at least one more, especially if the first child happens to be a girl. Each turning point and the rituals associated with them, emphasize (among many other things) the harmonizing of individual experiences and projects with more universal or natural processes. This is perhaps best symbolized in the experience of many "about to be married" couples that events have been taken out of their hands, that the form of the wedding, the persons to be invited, the money to be spent are all decisions made chiefly in response to "others", to kin, to parents, to neighbours, to "them".

This account is, of course, exaggerated although it does have its scholarly counterpart in sociologist's models of the "family life cycle" (Walker, 1977). Family life, in short, is said to consist of an orderly sequence of events which are understood as the cultural realizations of a natural order. It is clear that the effective linking of family processes with a natural order is much clearer in the case of women than with men. Graham has shown how this is achieved at times of pregnancy and makes a suggestive parallel between pregnancy and notions of spirit possession (Graham, 1976) while Macintyre shows how commonsense notions of motherhood and maternal instincts are overturned when the mother-to-be is found to be unmarried (Macintyre, 1976). Motherhood is clearly a much more tangible and powerful identity than fatherhood although it should be remembered that this too is sometimes popularly equated with proof of masculinity, the attainment of full male adulthood and of "settling down".

Against this simplified model of family processes we may place, in contrast, a model which is based upon ideas of personal, rational and informed choice at each stage or turning point. The best single symbol of this would probably be the birth-control pill (significantly and more acceptably labelled "family planning") enabling the process of child-birth to be harmonized with other projects, such as work or careers. Inevitably, this alternative model is not one that can be summarized as neatly as the former model. All the apparent branchings-off and dead-ends that appear as deviations from the conventional model of the "family life cycle" may be redefined as options which may be knowingly chosen by individuals. Such chosen and informed options would include the single status, single-parent families, childless couples and so on. More generally, this theme of rational choice or individual realization may be seen as a theme underlying many of the proposed alternatives to the nuclear family as we know it. Communes may appear, or be proposed as, viable alternatives to the quasi-inevitable bracketing of marriage and occupational career, while dual- or two-career families may be seen as attempts to overcome the equally apparently inevitable set of "either/ors" presented to the educated married woman. This is not to ignore the fact that members of many contemporary communes may view their collective projects as being more "in tune with nature" as compared with the artificialities of a rational, acquisitive culture; the point, however, is that such a "natural" option is chosen.

I have attempted to contrast two models of family processes, the one based upon an understanding in terms of a quasi-natural, inevitable and orderly sequence of events, the other based upon active, human control and individual choice. I suggest further that most of the proposed alternatives or modifications to the existing nuclear family are expressed in terms of a preference for the second model as against the first. It is now necessary to consider some difficulties with the notion of human control and choice as applied to family processes.

In the first place, there are difficulties arising out of the fact that the model deals with *individual* choice. At the most general level we should remind ourselves of what sociologists, following Weber, have called "the paradox of unintended consequences" the tendency for social events sometimes to be very different from what the individual participants, each pursuing rational courses of action, intended. In short, today's choices may become tomorrow's constraints. One example, as yet unrealized, is Etzioni's example of the possible social consequences that might follow were individual couples free to choose the sex of their children and tended, as would probably be the case, to favour the male sex (Etzioni, 1971; Rose and Hamner, 1976). Less speculatively, we may note how the pursuit of the goal of sexual freedom itself one of the main motives for rejecting the traditional family model, has produced a new set of constraints arising out of open-ended and ever-retreating standards of sexual attractiveness and success. Once again, the chief loser in this anomic race would appear often to be the woman.

Apart from the "paradox of unintended consequences", there are some more specific problems with the pursuit of individual goals in relation to family processes. The often repeated motives for entering communes or taking part in forms of group marriage to seek individual fulfilment or to realize one's potential, may be understood as *extensions* of the ethic of an advanced capitalist society rather than an articulated opposition to it. This is not entirely true, of course, and members of communes may elaborate an ethic of community, co-operation and sharing as well as, or instead of, a more simply individualistic ethic of self-realization. Yet the tension, sometimes the contradiction, between the ethic of self-fulfilment and the need for co-operation appears to be a major theme in the literature on contemporary communes. For the most part, the individualistic element appears dominant:

> Why do I live at Morning Star? I groove here. I feel myself at peace. I feel empathy (Quoted by Lamott, 1968, p. 133).

> Freedom is a . . . central value in the contemporary commune . . . the communes cherish the joy of brotherhood, but do not focus their lives completely on it (Zablocki, 1971, p. 167).

Outside the commune movement, of course, in the literature on revitalized and open marriages and families, the ethic of self-realization is much stronger. The conclusion of the O'Neill's *Open Marriage* perhaps expresses this in the most extreme terms:

> The peaks are there—you and your mate can ignore them, can huddle in the narrow valleys, or you can seek them out. You as a couple can be the

creators of a new life style for yourself and your mate, you alone can create the possibilities for transcendence (O'Neill and O'Neill, 1973, pp. 268–9).

The extent to which the pursuit of "possibilities for transcendence" in a marital enclave, seemingly detached from the multiplicity of pressing constraints in the world of work, is a solution or simply part of the problem is, to put it mildly, open to discussion. Work and occupational careers place powerful limitations on the extent of experimentation in alternative life-styles possible for a large section of the population.

Reference to economic constraints suggests further difficulties. In keeping with the overall title of this symposium it might be useful to consider the effect of these alternative ways of experiencing family life on wider patterns of inequalities namely those of sex and social class. In the case of sex, it can be suggested very broadly that while both men and women have benefited from the extension of personal choice and control into the family, they have not benefited equally. Holmstrom's study of "two-career families" shows, among other things, the limitations surrounding the joint pursuit of equality even under relatively favourable circumstances. The women tended to be more accommodating to the men in the question of where to live and when to move (although the husbands were sometimes significantly influenced in these matters by their wives' careers) and were more likely to fall foul of anti-nepotism rules than their spouses (Holmstrom, 1972). Generally, the relative equality of the two-career wives, such as the wives in the Rapoport's dual-career families (Rapoport and Rapoport, 1971), depended ultimately on the fortunate choice of the right husband. The O'Neill's model of "open marriage" looks highly egalitarian until it is realized that the emphasis throughout the book is on couples with little or no mention of children. Maureen Green notes, rather sharply:

> For the woman in charge of small children, 'open' marriage simply leaves her feeling draughtily exposed (Green, 1976, p. 24).

Abrams and McCulloch, in their survey of some British communes, conclude that these proposed alternatives to the family rarely make any serious attempt to tackle the mother-child relationship, one of the chief sources of sexual inequality within the "normal" family (Abrams and McCulloch, 1976). Speck's chapter heading "Pets on the periphery" summarizes the fate of many "chicks" in urban communes (Speck and Attneave, 1974) and other rural communes have been found to manifest a return to idealized frontier-type sexual divisions of labour, perhaps even a rejection of what might be seen as a relative confusion of sex-roles in the straight society (Downing, 1970; Kanter, 1973). One may also note the predominance of male gurus or charismatic leaders, the most extreme being Charles Manson, in contemporary communes.

A similar picture emerges in relation to social class. Holmstrom's "two-career families" enjoy the favourable and more flexible environments offered by academic or professional careers and again, like the dual-career families, rely on regular, paid domestic help. Bernard's favoured option of two part-time careers—the "shared-role pattern"—seems also to be modelled on the possibilities found in some professional careers (Bernard, 1973). It is difficult to imagine the O'Neill's "open marriage" flourishing anywhere other than relatively affluent residential suburbs and Speck's "retribalized" networks (where, in the course of network therapy, some forty or fifty persons gather in one private house) would appear to be similarly class-bound. Finally, repeated studies of contemporary communes in Britain and the United States show their members to be young, white and middle-class in origin (Abrams and McCulloch, 1976; Westhues, 1972). It might not be too fanciful to suggest the emergence of a new theme in social stratification and perhaps class antagonism, whereby one section of society increasingly enjoys the freedom to choose and evolve new "intimate life styles" while the other larger section of the population continues to be locked into the apparent inevitabilities of family life-cycles.

Conclusions

This theme of increasing choice in family matter is not, of course, a new one. Goode is not the only sociologist to have traced the growth of choice and control on the part of an evolving, conjugally-based family; choice in when and whom to marry, choice in the size of family, and choice in whether to end the marriage through divorce (Goode, 1970). Yet it may also be argued that these earlier extensions in the sphere of choice were in some measure consistent with and perhaps even supportive of the demands of an industrial economy. Undoubtedly some further changes will take place without their coming up against the constraints of the economy; the family or its alternatives can be seen as relatively autonomous institutions. Yet it is likely that large-scale extensions of experimentation in family living, particularly those experiments involving radical re-definitions of the role of women, will not be possible without wider economic changes. Until then, most purely individual or idiosyncratic attempts to reshape the constraints of family life will be more dependent upon the capitalist economy within which these experiments take place; and more dependent upon the maintenance of a mainstream pattern of nuclear family living, than will changes in the economic context depend upon experiment in family living.

Yet perhaps this is too pessimistic or perhaps, which is often the same thing, too utopian in that it awaits some future revolutionary change before further changes in the family can be put on the agenda. There are three reasons why it should be possible to conclude on a more optimistic note. In the first place we should not lose sight of the dialectic between individual experience and social change. Certainly, we can say that the search for alternative patterns of family or quasi-family living are shaped by and to some extent dependent upon the wider society in which these experiments take place; yet it is also true to argue that some of these experiments may become models for wider sections of the population and that a search for alternative patterns may also create demands for changes in areas outside the family. Thus, changes in the domestic division of labour that may result from an extension of employment opportunities to women may further create a greater demand for changes in the way in which work is organized.

In the second place, we should combine this analysis of relatively freely chosen family processes with our earlier analysis in terms of networks. Notions of "open marriage" or "open families" make more sense when they are seen not simply as purely individual experiments in personal growth but as part of an ever widening network of relationships. In short, we need to see what these families are "open" to. In contemporary society it is important to examine the networks of relationships that develop or are activated through various forms of community action or through persons coming together in the face of a particular obstacle or disability. Particularly valuable here are the experiences of various sections of the "women's movement".

Finally, and to return to the original point, perhaps the chief value in thinking about alternative social processes and social networks lies in the possibility it affords us to demystify the family, to see family relationships in the context of other relationships, to see their relative strengths and weaknesses without giving prior or unquestioned respect to a relationship simply because it is accorded the label "family". E. P. Thompson once wrote of the "enormous condescension of posterity" (Thompson, 1968, 13), referring to the process whereby the failures or blind-alleys of the past so readily become dismissed as irrational, foolish or quaint. Today, condescension does not wait for posterity; the simple words "fashionable" or "trendy" are enough. That individuals, couples or groups should, in the face of these labels, seek to improve and expand their lives and, in so doing, perhaps also provide a critique of contemporary society and its institutions should in itself be enough to encourage the rest of us to give them a sympathetic if not uncritical hearing. In listening, we may become aware of the possibilities within our own families and networks.

References

Abrams, P. and McCulloch, A. (1976). Men, women and communes. In *Sexual Divisions and Society: Process and Change*. Edited by D. L. Barker and S. Allen. London: Tavistock Publications.

Adams, R. N. (1960). An enquiry into the nature of the family. Reprinted in part in *Kinship*. Edited by J. Goody (1971). Harmondsworth, Middx.: Penguin Books.

Barker, D. L. and Allen, S. (Editors) (1976). *Sexual Divisions and Society: Process and Change*. London: Tavistock Publications.

Bernard, J. (1973). *The Future of Marriage*. London: Souvenir Press.

Borland, M. (Editor) (1976). *Violence in the Family*. Manchester: Manchester University Press.

Bott, E. (1971). *Family and Social Network*, (second edition), London: Tavistock Publications.

Bronfenbrenner, U. (1968). The changing soviet family. Reprinted in *The Nuclear Family in Crisis: The Search for an Alternative*. Edited by M. Gordon, 1972 New York: Harper and Row.

Cooper, D. (1972). *The Death of the Family*. Harmondsworth, Middx.: Penguin Books.

Davin, D. (1976). *Woman-Work*. Oxford: Clarendon Press.

Dickens, C. (1864). *Our Mutual Friend*. London: Dent and Sons (1907).

Downing, J. (1970). The tribal family and the society of awakening. In *The Family in Search of a Future*. Edited by H. A. Otto New York: Appleton-Century Crofts.

Etzioni, A. (1971). Sex control, science and society. In *Family in Transition*. Edited by A. Skolnick and J. Skolnick. Boston: Little Brown.

Folsom, J. K. (1934). *The Family: Its Sociology and Social Psychiatry*. New York: John Wiley and Sons.

Gardiner, J. (1975). Women's domestic labour. *New Left Review*, **89**, 47–58.

Geiger, H. K. (1968). *The Family in the Soviet Union*. Cambridge, Mass.: Harvard University Press.

Goode, W. J. (1970). *World Revolution and Family Patterns*. New York: Free Press.

Goode, W. J. (Editor) (1971). *The Changing American Family*. (New York Times Book). New York: Quadrangle Books.

Gordon, M. (Editor) (1972). *The Nuclear Family in Crisis: The Search for an Alternative*. New York: Harper and Row.

Graham, H. (1976). The social image of pregnancy: pregnancy as spirit possession. *The Sociological Review*, **24**, 291–308.

Green, M. (1976). *Goodbye Father*. London: Routledge and Kegan Paul.

Henry, J. (1972). *Pathways to Madness*. London: Jonathan Cape.

Holmstrom, L. L. (1972). *The Two-Career Family*. Cambridge, Mass.: Schenkman Publishing Company.

Ineichen, B. (1977). Youthful marriage: The vortex of disadvantage. (This volume).

Kanter, R. M. (1973). Family organisation and sex roles in American communes. In *Communes: Creating and Managing the Collective Life*. Edited by R. M. Kanter. New York: Harper and Row.

Laing, R. D. (1971). *The Politics of the Family and Other Essays*. London: Tavistock Publications.

Lamott, K. (1968). Doing their thing at Morning Star. Reprinted in part in *Communes: Creating and Managing the Collective Life*. Edited by R. M. Kanter (1973). New York: Harper and Row.

LeMasters, E. E. (1970). *Parents in Modern America*. Illinois: The Dorsay Press.

Litwak, E. and Szelenyi, I. (1969). Primary group structures and their functions: kin, neighbours and friends. *American Sociological Review*, **34**, 465–481.

Macintyre, S. (1976). Who wants babies? The social construction of 'instincts'. In *Sexual Divisions and Society: Process and Change*. Edited by D. L. Barker and S. Allen. London: Tavistock Publications.

Mintz, S. W. and Wolf, E. R. (1950). An analysis of ritual co-parenthood (*Compadrazgo*). Reprinted in part in *Kinship*. Edited by J. Goody (1971). Harmondsworth, Middx.: Penguin Books.

Mitchell, J. C. (Editor) (1969). *Social Networks in Urban Situations*. Manchester: Manchester University Press.

Oakley, A. (1974). *The Sociology of Housework*. London: Martin Robertson.

O'Neill, N. and O'Neill, G. (1973). *Open Marriage: A New Life Style for Couples*. London: Peter Owen.

Otto, H. A. (Editor) (1970). *The Family in Search of a Future*. New York: Appleton-Century-Crofts.

Powell, A. (1956–76). *A Dance to the Music of Time*. London: Heinemann.

Rapoport, R. and Rapoport, R. (1971). *Dual-Career Families*. Harmondsworth, Middx.: Penguin Books.

Rigby, A. (1974). *Alternative Realities*. London: Routledge and Kegan Paul.

Rose, H. and Hamner, J. (1976). Women's Liberation, reproduction and the technological fix. In *Sexual Divisions and Society: Process and Change*. Edited by D. L. Barker and S. Allen. London: Tavistock Publications.

Sandilands, J. (1976). Portrait of a generation: how sweet is 16? *Observer Magazine*, 14–23. 12th September.

Sennett, R. (1970). *Families Against the City*. Cambridge, Mass.: Harvard University Press.

Sennett, R. (1971). *The Uses of Disorder*. Harmondsworth, Middx.: Allen Lane. The Penguin Press.

Skolnick, A. (1973). *The Intimate Environment*. Boston: Little Brown.

Speck, R. V. (1972). *The New Families*. London: Tavistock Publications.

Speck, R. V. and Attneave, C. L. (1974). *Family Networks*. New York: Vintage Books.

Stacey, M. (1969). Family and household. In *Comparability in Social Research*. Edited by M. Stacey. London: Heinemann (Social Science Research Council).

Stoller, F. H. (1970). The intimate network of families as a new structure. In *The Family in Search of a Future*. Edited by H. A. Otto. New York: Appleton-Century-Crofts.

Talmon, Y. (1962). The family in a revolutionary movement—the case of the kibbutz in Israel. In *The Family: Its Structure and Functions* (second edition). Edited by R. L. Coser (1974). New York: Macmillan.

Thompson, E. P. (1968). *The Makings of the English Working Class*. Harmondsworth, Middx.: Penguin Books.

Veevers, J. E. (1973). Voluntarily childless wives: an exploratory study. Reprinted in *Intimacy, Family and Society*. Edited by A. Skolnick and J. Skolnick. Boston: Little Brown.

Walker, C. (1977). Some variations in marital satisfaction. (This volume).

Westhues, K. (1972). *Society's Shadow: Studies in the Sociology of Counter-Cultures.* Toronto: McGraw-Hill, Ryerson.

Yorburg, B. (1973). *The Changing Family.* New York: Columbia University Press.

Zablocki, B. (1971). Problems of anarchism on hippie communes. In *Communes: Creating and Managing the Collective Life.* Edited by R. M. Kanter (1973). New York: Harper and Row.

Author Index

Italic numbers indicate those pages where references are listed in full

Subject Index